*The Musick of the Mocking Birds,*
*the Roar of the Cannon*

William Winters

The

# *Musick*

of the Mocking Birds, the

# ROAR

of the Cannon

The Civil War Diary and Letters

of William Winters

*Edited by Steven E. Woodworth*

University of Nebraska Press

LINCOLN AND LONDON

⊗ The paper in this book meets the minimum
requirements of American National Standard
for Information Sciences—Permanence of Paper
for Printed Library Materials, ANSI Z39.48-1984.

Library of Congress Cataloging-in-Publication Data

Winters, William, 1830–

The musick of the mocking birds, the roar

of the cannon / William Winters;

edited by Steven E. Woodworth.

p.   cm.

Includes bibliographical references and index.

ISBN 0-8032-4773-7 (cloth: alk. paper)

1. Winters, William, 1830– Correspondence.

2. United States. Army. Indiana Infantry Regiment,

67th (1862–1864).   3. United States—History—

Civil War, 1861–1865—Personal narratives.

4. Indiana—History—Civil War, 1861–1865—

Personal narratives.   5. Soldiers—Indiana—

Bartholomew County—Correspondence.

6. Bartholomew County (Ind.)—Biography.

I. Woodworth, Steven E.   II. Title.

E506.5 6th   1998

973.7′472—dc21

98-15877

CIP

*In memory of Michael Joesph Quigley,*
*World War II veteran,*
*and dedicated to Liam Terrence Quigley,*
*the most recent generation of Americans.*
*May his and future generations honor*
*and respect in deep reverence*
*our country's heritage.*

# CONTENTS

# MAPS

Spring was on the land, and the Sixty-seventh Indiana Volunteer Infantry Regiment was marching off to war again. In the ranks, Sgt. William Winters, though on a destructive raid deep into enemy territory, a mission "to try to kill my fellow men," was nevertheless alive to the beauties of the land and the season around him. In his letters home he tried to describe one of those glorious southern springtides that for a season drive from the mind all memory of the South's raw, dripping winters or the fetid heat of its summers. Sights, sounds, and smells combined in a harmony of pleasant sensations, as Winters wrote of shrubs, flowers, and fragrances and noted that "the musick of the mocking birds" was now to be heard in the land.

That was just like William Winters, a mature father of three who went off to war and served through some of the conflict's most decisive campaigns but filled his letters home with far more about his surroundings and his comrades than about his battles and commanders. Winters's war was a journey of discovery into a culture and climate both different from and similar to his own, and his letters reflect his fascination with the contrasts he found—and perhaps as well his desire to focus on the beauties of nature around him as a relief from the dreary scenes of war in which he was a participant. No mockingbirds sang in Winters's "old Hoosier home" or among the "pineclad hills" of his boyhood home in New England, but their song was common in the Deep South. "The musick of the mocking birds" would have been perhaps as common as any acoustic feature of a world so enchanting that Winters thought he might very much like to live there, but for the discordant and sinister note of its being "cursed with rebels and slavery." The mocking irony of human wickedness in the midst of creation's beauties was rarely lost on Winters and characterized his Civil War odyssey.

William Winters Jr. was born in Connecticut in 1830. As a young man he came—possibly in company with other members of his family—to Cincinnati, Ohio, where in 1853 he married Harriet J. Smith, a twenty-year-old native of Ohio. The new Mrs. Winters generally went by the name Hattie, and in his Civil War letters to her, William addressed her most often simply as "hat." During the mid-1850s the couple moved to Hawes Creek Township in Bartholomew County, Indiana, southeast of Indianapolis. William worked as a saddle and harness maker, and the family grew. In 1857 their first child, Edith, was born. Two years later came another girl, Effah Mae, whom William usually called simply "May." Early in 1860 yet a third female child, this one named Maggie, made her appearance in the Winters household. By that time William had become an established citizen in Hawes Creek Township, and in 1859 his name had appeared along with those of twenty-three other residents on a petition for the incorporation of their new town, to be christened "Hope."[1]

It was a name fully in character with the optimistic, forward-looking confidence of Winters and his fellow townsmen. For the Winters family in particular, the 1860s were to be a time of steadfast hope tempered by deep sorrow. By 1862 little Maggie was gone, apparently carried off by one of the many diseases that then stalked early childhood. The following year another child was born, a boy this time, named after his father.

Meanwhile war had come to America, and thousands of young men had marched off to the fighting. While battles raged in Kentucky, Tennessee, and Virginia and along the southern coast and the Mississippi River, while Ulysses S. Grant won a reputation and George B. McClellan lost one, William Winters remained at home with his family. By July 1, 1862, President Abraham Lincoln had recognized that the war was not, as it had appeared that spring, on the verge of successful termination. Determined to see it through to victory, the president called on the governors of the Union states for three hundred thousand more volunteers to fill out the nation's depleted armies and "bring this unnecessary and injurious Civil War to an end." It was this appeal that inspired James Sloan Gibbons's poem (subsequently set to music) "We Are Coming Father Abraham, Three Hundred Thousand More." In a last great surge of patriotic recruiting fervor—before the adoption of draft- and bounty-driven methods of filling the ranks—the country responded to Lincoln's call.[2]

Among the new regiments formed from these "three hundred thousand more" was the Sixty-seventh Indiana. Recruited in seven counties of central and southern Indiana during the summer of 1862, the regiment assembled in Madison, Indiana, on the Ohio River between Cincinnati and Louisville. There the various companies were sworn into Federal service on August 19 and 20, for a term of three years. From Bartholomew County, where local citizens pledged to support the families of any who should enlist, came Company I, and among them was William Winters. The new soldiers were farm boys, by and large, who averaged twenty years of age, ten years younger than Winters.[3]

And so began the Civil War experience of this small-town saddle and harness maker and father. He was a steady letter writer, like many soldiers using the activity as both a pastime and a relief from homesickness. He did not bother himself with such trivialities as punctuation, and virtually all of the punctuation in the pages that follow has been added for ease of reading. The scholar who wishes to know what Winters's script looked like as it came from his pen needs only to disregard all punctuation. Winters also seems not to have felt bound by any conventional rules of capitalization, except for the pronoun *I*. Otherwise he capitalized or not (usually not) as suited him. Spelling also could be an expression of his individuality, but that was not so unusual in those days. Andrew Jackson, who was president when William Winters was born, once observed that he pitied a man who could think of only one way to spell a word. Winters was not so limited and not infrequently spelled a word at least two different ways within the same sentence. His spelling and capitalization are faithfully reproduced in the pages that follow, with the use of brackets kept to a minimum—generally only when absolutely necessary to avoid confusion.

For all his idiosyncratic use of written English, Winters was about as literate as the average enlisted man. Other wartime writings may read more like fine literature, but such usually stem from the pens of officers. Winters's is the voice of the common soldier, of one of those who "left their plows and workshops" to save the Union, and this lends his thoughts and observations a particular interest.

In chapter introductions, endnotes, and occasionally inserted connecting narrative, I have endeavored to explain Winters's statements and place them in context. Like many Civil War soldiers, he did not fill his letters with accounts of the great commanders and their strategies nor with the tactical details of the battles and skirmishes in which he was involved. The former he could not possibly have known, the latter he—like many others—usually assumed that his readers would already have learned from the newspapers. In my additions to this manuscript, my goal is to give the reader the knowledge that the Civil War soldier expected in his correspondents and to help the modern student of the war understand and appreciate the circumstances in which the various letters were written.

The original manuscript copies of Winters's wartime letters are in the possession of his descendant Michael G. Quigley of Garden Grove, California, who graciously permitted me to use them in this project. The original diary no longer exists, but Mr. Quigley allowed me to use a handwritten copy made by Winters's granddaughter. I would like to acknowledge the kind assistance of Mr. Quigley and Mary Janet Fehr Quigley, another descendant of William Winters, as well as John W. Hamblen, Professor Emeritus of the University of Missouri–Rolla and Librarian of the Bartholomew County Historical Society.

*The Musick of the Mocking Birds,*
*the Roar of the Cannon*

ONE

# *"An Army amongst Them"*

The newly sworn-in Hoosiers of the Sixty-seventh might have been as green as Indiana grass that summer, but a crisis was brewing in Kentucky, just across the Ohio River, and the War Department hastily threw the new regiment and others like it from all over the Midwest into the thick of the campaign. The Sixty-seventh hastily organized, drew uniforms and equipment, and marched down to the steamship landing for transportation to the seat of war. "Uncle Sam," the regimental historian later observed, "had urgent need of us."[1]

Arriving in Munfordville, Kentucky, they found elements of several other regiments defending fortifications on the south bank of the Green River. From this period dates William Winters's first letter. Characteristically, his interest was in the countryside, the people of the region, and their reactions to the "army amongst them."

Camp Jackson, Munfordville,
K.Y., Aug. 31st, [18]62

Dear wife, it is sunday to day in all the world, but in camp and here it is the same as any other day. almost the only differance is we know that it is the sabath. there is the same noise, bustle, and confusion as

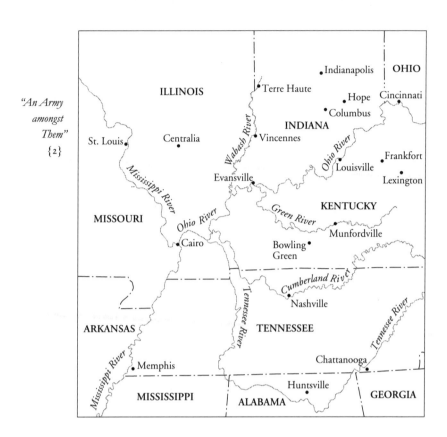

Indiana and the upper South

on any other of the seven, but we are all well and enjoying ourselves as well as we can. I have just eat my diner and the balance of our mess are washing the dishes. I do the most of the cooking as the rest of our mess say they cant cook.

We are situated on the top of a hill on the bank of green river and in sight of the towns of woodsonville and Munfordville and in one of the poorest countrys that I ever saw.[2] there is not a spear of grain or a rick of straw to be seen in any direction and not a plow at work, but the people dont seem to mind it much. it may be that they have got so used to haveing an army amongst them that they dont notice it any more. the country is very rough and broken, and I dont think it has rained any here for the last three months, as the ground is perfectly parched up. the grass looks as dry as if there had never been any rain since the world commenced.[3]

we have all kinds of reports here about old Morgan.[4] the last is this morning that he was down about glasgow, a town of about three or four hundred inhabitants. it is about sixteen miles from here.[5] they say he had some two thousand men with him now, but if there is no more than his forces comes against us we dont care, as we have some twenty five hundred here now, as we were reinforced with one more regiment on yesterday and two more peices of artilery and we expect two more regiments on to day or to morow and four more canon, and we are throwing up brest works and building a stockade, and I think that if we can get the works done that we have commenced before he trys to take us, he will meet a last repulse for this life.

the war department are impressing all the negroes to work on the fortifications that are in the country. they have some fifty-five contrysbands[6] at work here now and colonal Emerson[7] says they must do the work and save the men, but it makes some of these old fellows around here awfull mad to think that they must give up their hands to work for unkle sam when they dont like him a single bit. and yesterday they commenced impresing horses and oxen to work on the works to save the soldiers. we have our watter hauled here to our tents now, and it saves us a heap of hard work, for it was an awfull job to carry watter more than a half mile in buckets, camp kettles, and coffe pots to drink and cook with. we had a nice lot of fresh beef dealt out to us to day, the first that I have had since I came into camp. we have plenty of work and plenty to eat if we only had a good way of cooking it, but we will soon get used to it. I would like to have some of your bread for supper to night. we have crackers instead of bread, but I think they intend to change it as often as they can.[8]

[remainder of letter missing]

Winters's first taste of combat came just two weeks to the day after he wrote this letter. On Sunday morning, September 14, Confederate brigadier general James R. Chalmers assaulted the Federals at Munfordville.[9]

Inside the Federal works, the Sixty-seventh Indiana held a powerful earthwork called Fort Craig, on the extreme left of the Union line near the village of Woodsonville. The hard work on the entrenchments Winters mentioned, both by the soldiers and by commandeered slaves, now paid off for the new troops. Though it was their first fight, the men of the Sixty-seventh found the job simple enough for their level of training, as they stood behind their breastworks and fired at the oncoming Rebels. They also found that they possessed skills and aptitude for the job. It was "Hoosier squirrel hunt drill," recalled one participant. Officers seemed to have more difficulty guessing appropriate behavior. Maj. Augustus H. Abbot of the Sixty-seventh leapt atop the parapet shouting, "Shoot low," and was promptly cut down by a Confederate bullet.[10]

When the Confederates retreated, the green Hoosiers of the Sixty-seventh had been seasoned by combat, and a serious enough fight it was, while it lasted. They noted with pride that their flag had been pierced by 146 enemy bullets.[11]

Two days later, Confederate general Braxton Bragg showed up with his whole army. That was more than the Munfordville garrison could handle, and the Federals, including the Sixty-seventh Indiana, surrendered, marched out "with all the honors of war, drums beating and colors flying," stacked their arms, and became prisoners of war.[12]

The Sixty-seventh Indiana had taken 931 officers and men to Munfordville. One officer, Major Abbot, and 10 enlisted men had been
killed in the battle of September 14. The remainder, including the 32
wounded men, were surrendered on the seventeenth. Their captivity
was short-lived, however. Paroled the next day, they were free to go
but forbidden to serve against the Rebels until duly exchanged. Leaving Munfordville, the column of parolees marched southward to meet
Buell's army, moving up from Nashville. After reporting and drawing
supplies, they marched north again to the Ohio River at Louisville,
crossed back into their home state at New Albany, and after a few
encouraging words from Governor Oliver P. Morton, proceeded by
rail to Indianapolis, where they arrived on the last day of September.
There the men were granted four-week furloughs and shortly found
themselves back at the homes they had left less than two months
before.[13]

Thus this first chapter of William Winters's Civil War experience
was short, carried him only about 150 miles from home, and pro-
duced only a single letter. The next was to be far different.

# TWO

# *"The Grand Panorama before Me"*

By the first of November the furloughs were over and the men of the Sixty-seventh Indiana were back in camp. This was Camp Morton, near Indianapolis, and for the Sixty-seventh it was "parole camp," where they would wait, unequipped and with little to do, until they could be officially exchanged. The idleness and bleak weather were bad for morale.

The familiar if demoralizing camp routine was broken toward the end of November by the announcement that the regiment had been exchanged. The men once again drew weapons from the ordnance department. Drill and instruction replaced idleness. Then, on December 5, 1862, the Sixty-seventh Indiana boarded the train that was to carry it on the first leg of its journey back into the theater of conflict.[1]

Their target was the Confederate Mississippi River bastion of Vicksburg, Mississippi. Conquering this stronghold was a task assigned to Maj. Gen. Ulysses S. Grant, and the Sixty-seventh Indiana was among the troops he would use for the purpose. First under Grant's subordinate Maj. Gen. William Tecumseh Sherman and then under Maj. Gen. John A. McClernand, another of Grant's lieutenants, the Sixty-seventh took part in the long, strenuous, alternately heart-breaking and exhilarating, ultimately successful campaign.

The early stages, in December 1862 and January 1863, featured vigorous movements and both victories and defeats. In December, Grant took a force under his own command southward through central Mississippi to come at Vicksburg by the back door while Sherman, with a force that included the Sixty-seventh, came straight down the Mississippi to try to kick in the front door. The plan failed. Confederate cavalry cut Grant's vulnerable overland supply line, forcing him to retreat, and Sherman's frontal assault faced impossible terrain. The resulting battle of Chickasaw Bayou had a predictable result, though the Sixty-seventh escaped the worst of the carnage. Several days later, McClernand superseded Sherman in command along the river and, at Sherman's suggestion, took the army on a profitable river-borne excursion against Confederate Fort Hindman on the Arkansas River at a place known as Arkansas Post, a constant threat to Union river-borne operations against Vicksburg until it was taken by the January 1863 expedition. The successful attack represented the Sixty-seventh's third experience in pitched battle.

During this stage of his service, Winters kept a diary, which is presented here with his letters interspersed at the appropriate places. In both he reflected on the terrain and the people he encountered more than on the details of the battlefields. He wrote with awe and pride of the magnificent spectacle presented by the assembled fleet of gunboats and transports that set out for Vicksburg. "A fitting sight for an artist's pencil," he called it. Clearly he was proud to be part of the forces of this mighty republic.

He was also deeply impressed, however, by the destructiveness of the army toward civilian property. When the Sixty-seventh had begun its enforced pause in military operations the previous September, the war was in the process of transition from a limited struggle for limited goals to a profoundly destructive conflict aimed at the very heart of the Southern social system. Only a few days after the Sixty-seventh had marched, unarmed, northward toward its parole camp, Lincoln had issued his Preliminary Emancipation Proclamation. Engaged now in a war to end slavery, Federal forces had little hope of conciliating Southerners through mild treatment. The task that remained was simple and brutal: to bring the South to its knees. That sometimes meant burning houses from which (or from the vicinity of which) shots had been fired into passing Union steamboats. It often meant destroying railroads, food supplies, and whatever public or private property might in any way sustain the Confederate war effort.[2]

Toward both the destruction and the blacks whose plight was the cause of the war, Winters was ambivalent. The blacks were a curiosity, to which he referred with the racial epithets that were typical of his day, but slavery, he repeatedly implied, was an evil system. Toward the destruction of private property, he was even more ambivalent. He sometimes viewed it as a matter of justice to perfidious traitors. "We are paying them back," he wrote. At such times he could take pride in the army's deeds, noting once, "I guess we left our mark last night." Yet at other times, destroying property was a downright tiresome chore, and at still others, a thing of which he disapproved. The troops were "burning cotton & corn by the hundreds of thousands of dollars worth," he wrote after one particularly thorough session, "something that I consider wrong." Yet it is never quite clear whether he felt the wrong was in depriving rebellious owners of their property or in wasting perfectly good supplies that ought to have been used by the Union army.

Winters's concern for his children affords us rare glimpses into several aspects of mid-nineteenth-century life, particularly the normally invisible world of children and the family. William urged Hattie to tell their two daughters "that Pa says for them to be good girls," not an unusual paternal wish, but he added, "for they may never see their father again." This touched on nineteenth-century ideas about death in giving special significance to any final message from the departing. If Edith and Effah Mae did not see their father again, if he perished in the army, then his final admonition to "be good girls" would take on added emotional impact. The statement may also have referred to a hope that the family might be reunited in heaven—even if its members might not see one another again on earth—if they lived their lives as Christians, something that Winters no doubt included within the concept of being "good girls."

Friday, Dec. 5, [18]62

struck tents today for Dixie and marched to the depot. On the Terre Haute and Indpls [Indianapolis] RR. Passed Greencastle & Terre Haute the same night. Waked up this morning in Illinois. Passed through the most level & inviting country today that I ever saw in the west. saw six deer sporting on the prairie & saw some prairie on fire on a small scale. some of the towns are very pretty & well laid out. left the T.H. & I [rail]road today & switched off on the Illinois Central [rail]road for Cairo. lost one man from Co. —— of our regiment by accident trying to get aboard the train as also did the 89[th Indiana] reg[iment].

Sunday, [December] 7, [1862]

Arrived at Cairo this morning at 2 o'clock & marched down & got aboard US Steamer Universe for Memphis. Slept the balance of the night on board steamer. got up this morning & went uptown to see the sights. saw some rebble officers, & it made me mad to see how they tryed to put on the style in a free state. also saw rebble privates that were taken prisoner, also some that diserted from Brags army that took us at Munfordsville. they pretended to want to enlist in the union army, but I wouldn't believe them under oath. left Cairo this afternoon at four o'clock and ran down to Columbus [Kentucky] & landed for a few minutes & then ran down the river a short distance & landed on the Missouri shore for the night

Monday, [December] 8, [1862]

Today we saw several boats. the river looks quite natural to me in some places. ran down to fort Pillow today & laid by for the night. wrote a letter to my wife [not found].

Tuesday, [December] 9, [1862]

left fort Pillow this morning & worked about two hours to make a kettle of coffee, then eat our breakfast & went up on the hericane deck to take a view of the country. saw quite a number of duck, geese, & brauts. several of the points looked familiar to me. saw a good deal of sugar cane. arrived at Memphis at one o'clock, landed & put on napsacks & accouterments to leave the boat but were ordered to stay aboard until tomorrow. saw some of the twelfth [Indiana] that were paroled since they came here. Finished a letter to my wife & mailed it [not found]. health good since I have been out this time.

Wednesday, [December] 10, [1862]

Went guard this morning & left the boat for camp about 1 o'clock. after got to camp went on guard. herd the Col. say that we would probably stay here this winter.

Thursday, [December] 11, [1862]

Came of[f] guard this morning. somehow took cold last night & coughed more today than I have for two years.

Friday, [December] 12, [1862]

Went out to drill this morning, the first time since we came here. after dinner went on grand review down through the streets of Memphis. had a view of the city. it has some splendid buildings & some fine private residence. the streets are all to narrow for a fine appearance. saw some bold ones here in crinoline.

Sunday, [December] 14, [1862]

Things today are about the same as Sundays generally in camp, but little like Sunday, as the Sabath is no more than any other day in the army.

Monday, [December] 15, [1862]

Today was a day to be remembered. this morning it rained & blowed & some of our tent stakes pulled up & in came wind & rain &

up we got & out to restake. went back & the tent leaked. the boys swore & laughed. some wished that they was at home & so did I. rained so hard that we got no breakfast or dinner. slacked up in time for supper. got some plank & straw for our tents & things look comfortable. things all wet yet. got marching orders for next thursday & ordered to cook seven days rations, destination unknown but suposed to be Vicksburgh.

Thursday, [December] 18, [1862]
Today I got of[f] guard & tryed my hand at target shooting with the company. Co. I [was] a peach for today, knocked the target all to peices.

Friday, [December] 19, [1862]
Today Wes[3] through [threw] up his commission as cook for the happy family, and we had quite a time, some of the boys showing the principles that make a raskle. Wes was quite sick today but is better tonight. Prospect of moving for Vicksburgh tomorrow. Wrote a letter to my wife tonight, also saw Hen McGlocklin & Jim Hudson from the 83d Ohio. The boys in our mess are playing euchre [a card game] as usual tonight.

In Camp, Near Memphis
Dec. 19th, [18]62
Dear wife, I will take this opportunity of writing again, as it may be the last time that I will have the opportunity of writing for a good while and perhaps for ever. We are on the eve of leaving for Vicksburg. We are making every preporation for a heavey engagement and a terible strugle, and many of us will never come back. I hope that I will be lucky enough to come home safe, but we dont know who will be the unlucky one.

We have had a verey good time since we have been here. we drilled allmost constantly. We have been practising target shooting for a couple of days and will continue to do so while we stay here. We have had fine weather for the most of the time since we have been in camp here. the wether is warm and pleasant and everey thing looks spring

like. Well, hat, I must tell you that I saw Henry McGlocklin and Jim
Hudson, and Elijah McGlocklin is here. I havent seen him yet. they
are in the 83 Ohio and in the same Brigade with us and will go down
the River with us.[4]

Wes was over to their Regiment and saw a lot of Cincinnati boys that
he knew. I havent had the time to go yet. Jim Hudson has been sick, but
he was a goodeal [good deal] better today and come over here to see
us, but wes was down in town. wes is not verey well. he has quit cooking and will come home, I guess, when we leave here, which I think will
be in a day or two, as our fleet is here and waiting for everey thing to be
got ready. I havent seen it, but wes told me that there was a hundred
boats, if not more, laying in the River waiting. we cant get any news
here untill it is four or five days old. Wes got a letter that Mary Jane
wrote to him before we left Indanoples [Indianapolis]. I sent you all
the money that I could after I got what [I] have [i.e., what I need]. I will
send you all that I draw the next time we are paid of[f], as I will make
out on what I can make at cooking if I live,[5] which I hope I will. I hope
that we will stay here long enough to hear from you, as this makes five
letters that I have written since I left home. I heard that tom quillen
was dead and Columbus Everet,[6] one of our Company that we left at
home when we left. we have got two boys that are quite sick. they are
both from the neighborhood of Hartsville,[7] Sim Blankenbaker[8] and
Henry Case.[9] Jim israiel[10] is in the guard house perfectly worthless.

I will try to write again if we dont leave tomorow or day after. give
my love to all. tell Edith and May that Pa says for them to be good
girls, for they may never see their father again.[11] Kiss them and Will
for me from your affectionate husband, Wm Winters

O how I wish I was at home to night. good by.


Saturday, [December] 20, [1862]

Today we struck tents for a move. cooked some rations for tomorrow. left camp for the boat about four o'clock and got on board after
dark. name of boat J. C. Pringle, a sternwheel.[12] the boys are all very
anxious to hear the particulars of the Fredericksburg fight.[13] if favorable to our forces it will have a good effect on this expedition & if not I

think it will make a failure of it. today had a council with Wes to know how he should proceed, & he concluded to go to Helena [Arkansas] with us.

Sunday, [December] 21, [1862]

This morning got up & washed without soap. Jo Gambold[14] went ashore & made some coffee for the mess. eat our breakfast & went out on the guard to take ——. wrote this sitting crosslegged like a tailor. just finished some checker men. Field McCalip[15] & Wes are playing on the top of a cartridge box that Wes cut a bord on. just leaving the city & streched out before me is one of the grandest spectakles to be seen—fifteen boats all with colors flying & covered with men all dressed in uniforms & cheering each other as they pass, a fitting sight for an artist's pencil.

must go make some coffee for supper. made coffee & called mess. No. 5 all eat supper up on huricane deck to see the country beyond. four boats bound up[river].

Monday, [December] 22, [1862]

Waked up this morning at Friears Point.[16] went up on deck & had the pleasure [of seeing?] the fire surpent devour some rebel houses. some of the boys got ribbons, books, paper, [illegible] stands, & some checkers. the fleet burned some 7 or 8 buildings & tore two to save some others. the inhabitants here fired into the Saturn some ten days ago, & we are paying them back. there is a fleet of some forty or fifty boats here now & more to come. we are just leaving & the sight is beautiful to see so many boats all under way at the same time. I saw a number of places that had been burned leaving nothing but the chimneys standing. I saw more blackbirds this evening than I ever saw in my life before. we have stopped for the night at a bend in the river some fifteen miles above Napoleon [Arkansas].[17]

Tuesday, [December] 23, [1862]

Started out this morning with the same grand panorama before me, the river covered with boats. passed Napoleon about nine o'clock.

saw several nigers this morning with their bundles hailing the boats to be taken aboard. saw the remains of the place on the oposite side from Napoleon. fire has done the work—nothing left but chimneys. just landed at Gasters landing. the fleet behind us landing on the opposite side. I must go ashore & make some coffee for dinner. well I have made coffee & eat my dinner consisting of hard crackers & coffee & now I will go out & see what I can see. well I have been ashore & seen the elephant.[18] Wes ordered to carry rails to cut for wood. done so. load aboard & concluded to quit. some of the boys of some of the other regiments burned a couple of houses as did the fleet on the other side of the river. we took a prisoner here, got three rifles & one shotgun with him. he was took to headquarters but don't know what was done with him. heard a rumor that forrests[19] cavalry was at Memphis, also heard that memphis has been taken since we left. don't believe the yarn. some of the boys got some chickens & turkeys, had to go to the Col. for it & got the devil.[20] supper time. we stay here to night. saw Elijah McGlocklin & Gerome Bryant—both well.

Wednesday, [December 24, 1862]

This morning the fleets have increased. the 131st Illinois had a fatal accident. while on picket duty last night one of their men carelessly went outside the line without leave & when he came back was shot by his own men suposing him to be an enemy. he received six balls. the river is quite foggy this morning. We have not started yet—nine o'clock. we are out upon the ocean sailing among the biggest fleet that ever went down this [river] or ever will again. I guess we left our mark last night. wherever a division landed, the hand of the incendiary was at work. saw some spanish moss today, the first I have seen on the trip.

Thursday, [December] 25, [1862]

Christmas morning

This morning got up Milligan's bend,[21] went ashore, made some coffee, and fried some meat for breakfast and got orders to fall into line for a scout. Started about 9 o'clock back into the country. Marched all day untill 7 o'clock & then went on guard. Passed through a rich country. [illegible] leaves plenty. Saw lots of cotton & corn. the niggers all welcomed us as we passed. my feet was never so sore in my life & I am awfull tired.

Friday, [December] 26, [1862]

This morning [I] came off guard & saw the effects of fire. We burned the Railroad bridge & tore up the track & burned some cotton & then got ready to go back to the boats & was ordered to stay, had not done our work. Finished our work of distruction by burning cotton & corn by the hundreds of thousands of dollars worth, something that I consider wrong. Marched back to the boats today & thought that I would never get there. My feet wore out & I was sick at my stomach & came very near fainting. had to lay down—never was so wore out in all my life. Got on board the boat again about 11 o'clock & layed down exhausted, to rest.

Saturday, [December] 27, [1862]

Got up this morning awful sore. drank some coffee, wrote a short letter home [not found] too late to get it of[f], as we was starting for some point further down the river. We have just rounded up into the mouth of the Yazoo river. Twenty five gunboats & some mortar boats are lying here ready for action. We have just landed some six or 8 miles above the mouth of the river—orders to cook 2 days rations & take one blanket for a march again. Reported myself to the doctor & got excused from duty until tomorrow—marching orders suspended until tomorrow. One of our gunboats [was] fired into yesterday by the rebels here. The boys are all just ordered out again—the most of them had turned in for the night & had to roll out in double quick.

Sunday, [December] 28, [1862]

Got up this morning early. slept but little. Everything was bustle & confusion all night. It is just getting daylight. I am ready once more for the fray. The roar of artillery is plain & the faint sound of musketry tells plainly that the ball is opened for the morning, in line of battle before the bluffs back of Vicksburg. Passed along the whole line. saw a good many wounded & several killed. One of Co. C of our regiment just killed by a cannon ball.[22] Firing gradually ceasing; night is putting an end to the fratricidal scenes of Sunday. This is the second Sunday fight I have seen. Heard today that Gen. L. Smith was mortally wounded today.[23]

Monday, [December] 29, [1862]

The ball has again opened. we are in the same position today as yesterday. Our forces took a battery of five guns from the rebbels on yesterday & one of four the day before. Saw something resembling turnips yesterday in full bloom—did not stop to see what it was. There has been some hard fighting to our left this morning, some of the hottest work that I ever want to see. Darkness is setting in & still the conflict rages on our left. It is commencing to rain & bids fair to make a bad night.

Tuesday, [December] 30, [1862]

Got up this morning, the old position we have occupied for the last three days. this morning I am about half of my body sopping wet. had to get up in the night & get some small cane to keep me up out of the water. rained all night. went out & shot my gun off & wiped it out. saw some rebels on the hill. we have just changed our position but what for I don't know unless to get the men out of the mud & filth. the sun has begun to shine giving us a chance to dry. this turns out to be so in part. one rumor says that the rebels were a going to shell the woods where we were. it is sundown & we have just eat our supper, fixed us a nest like the swine does by piling leaves up. we have made but little advance yet.

Wednesday, [December 31, 1862]

This morning we are on picket. we have had orders not [to] shoot at the enemy on any account as we are colecting our dead & wounded. some of the pickets have taken advantage of the truce & laid down their guns & met halfway & are now talking together & shaking hands & drinking. there is quite a squad of them talking in plain sight of my post now. we have had no fighting today of any consequence both being preparing for the morow. our forces sent in a flag of truce & demanded a surender & the rebels asked for a cessation of hostillities for twenty four hours which we granted taking advantage of the truce to bring out two 30 & four 20 pound & 6 ten pound rifled parot guns & succeed in planting all of them last night.

Thursday, Jan. 1, [18]63 New Year

This morning I was cold, damp, & tired, having stood picket 24 hours without being relieved. the truse still exists, & the scene is strangely quiet. we have all kinds of rumors but nothing reliable. we have not heard from home since leaving [for] Vicksburgh. firing with artillery is going on this afternoon at long range, both sides trying to find the others strong points. we have made no advance as yet of importance.

well, one more move that nobody knows anything about. we had just got to bed last night when we were called up & told to pack everything to march. got ready & came back to the boats & went to bed expecting to wake up in the Mississippi, but here we are yet & will be I guess.

Friday, [January] 2, 1863

Got up this morning & was disapointed to find myself in the same place I was last night. I expected to leave for some other point. just got an order to put on our belts & cartridge boxes & be ready to march in five minutes if necessary. did not go out but the fleet did. left the Yazoo river & landed at Milicans bend in the ships.

Saturday, [January] 3, [1863]

This morning it is raining hard & has rained the most of the night. I saw Ed Gorden last night. he is with the 83 Ohio as ambulance master. he is in fine trim, he says. we changed landings today again. we are now laying at Milicans town. it has rained nearly all day, & everything is in an awfull nasty condition. I believe I will write tonight as I hear there will be a chance to send up the river tomorrow. our company officers are all sick & have been for some time.

Sunday, [January] 4, [1863]

This morning Wes & I went ashore & made some coffee for the mess. the mud is awful deep up the bank. the report is we go into camp here. heard from the upper country last night, the first since leaving memphis & the news is bad. the boys are comenting on it in every way. I have just received a letter from my wife & cant account for not getting more. we have just got orders to clean up the boat, as we are going to Memphis again.

well we are landed once more but did not stay landed very long as we are now on our way up the river again. received a letter from home today—all well.

Monday, [January] 5, [1863]

This morning woke up & found the boat in motion. ran all night. no chance to get breakfast & went on guard without. had an accident on board today. lost a man overboard today. he was from newbern, name E. McCombs.[24] We are still bound up. laid by for most of the night. outran everything on river yesterday.

Tuesday, [January] 6, [1863]

Off guard again. company K lost a man last night by death. we have done nothing today of amount. ran about 25 miles today & waited the balance of the day. 9 o'clock. just came back from burying another of Co. K men that died since dark.

Wednesday, [January] 7, [1863]

This morning I am about half sick. wooding,[25] yet left the landing about 2 o'clock & are having quite a race [with] the USOND [another steamboat]. we have been running side by side for about an hour, but she has just gave up the race and dropped back.

Thursday, [January] 8, [1863]

This morning we are at the mouth of White river[26] & waiting for something, but nobody knows what.

well, we are bound for White river. one of the most interesting sights that a man can behold, the river perfectly crowded with boats in the misty twilight, all aparently aproaching some dreaded spot.

Friday, [January] 9, [1863]
Today we came up White river to a Rebel fort & prepared to make an attack.

Saturday, [January] 10, [1863]
Today the troops all disembarked for the field of action. have heard cannonading at several different times today. was detailed for hospital nurse on thursday & have been serving in that capacity since.

Sunday, [January] 11, [1863]
This morning have been in hospital all morning. the discharge of artillery is to be heard, but no small arms [are] to [be] heard.

well, the day is ended, & we have the field with between 5 & 8000 prisoners, but the fight was a hard one.

Monday, [January] 12, [1863]
Today has been one of bustle & confusion—nothing of importance only the dressing of wounds.

Tuesday, [January] 13, [1863]
Today there has been a general fixing up to leave again for some point either up or down the Mississippi, don't know which. saw three boats loaded with rebel prisoners bound for the upper country I believe. heard a paper read last night, the first paper I have heard read for some time.[27]

Wednesday, [January] 14, [1863]
Today I have performed the same old routine of duties that I have been performing for the last week.

Thursday, [January] 15, [1863]
This morning it is snowing quite hard & the ground is covered with a mantle of milky whiteness & all the boys are shivering & kicking to

keep their toes warm. I just asked an old darkey if it was common to have so much snow, & he said he never knew of its snowing so much or being so cold in his life.

Friday, [January] 16, [1863]
Today we ran down to the Mississippi again. still cold & blustery. it snowed all night last night again. the men are getting very tired of this boat ride & wish to be on shore a while again.

Saturday, [January] 17, [1863]
Well, here we are again at the city of Napoleon, Ark. I have just taken a stroll through the streets of this much begrimed place of misery. saw some of the troops enjoying themselves in the deserted domiciles of their enemies as there is but two or three families of women & children left in the town.

Sunday, [January] 18, [1863]
Today we have done nothing but shift about & get ready. Wes started for home today on board the Luzern. we lost Dick Hauser yesterday on the oposite side of the river.[28]

Monday, [January] 19, [1863]
Left Napoleon, ran down a short distance, & laid by for the night. Left five more of our boys at Napoleon.

Tuesday, [January] 20, [1863]
Started of[f] this morning. everything was in confusion but finealy got strait again. Stopped at Spanish Moss bend & wooded. Stopped again a short distance below. boys went out—our mess got 7 chickens, very fat.

Wednesday, [January] 21, [1863]
Off again this morning. Again ran down to the head of Milligans bend & landed. stayed about two hours & droped down about 15 miles & landed for the night.

# THREE

# "The Mournfull Call of the Sick"

When Grant's December 1862 attempt to take Vicksburg failed, the Union general determined to try again, this time by moving directly down the Mississippi River to a position above the fortress town and trying one means after another for coming at its defenses until he found one that brought success. For the Sixty-seventh Indiana and the other soldiers of the Army of the Tennessee, this was to mean three months of camping in the cold rain and mud among the swamps of the low-lying country near the river. For these midwesterners— chilled, damp, filthy, discouraged at the seeming futility of their efforts, and stalked by numerous and deadly diseases—the winter months of 1863 were indeed the times that tried men's souls.

For none was it more trying than the Hoosiers of the Sixty-seventh Indiana. They were as yet relatively new and had not yet completed the experience of "seasoning," the winnowing by disease and disability that reduced the average Civil War regiment to half its original strength, usually before it smelled its first hostile powder smoke. Detailed for duty at a field hospital as a military nurse, Winters was in a prime position to witness the parade of misery that filled these months. Indeed, his own health was none too good, and this seems to have had much to do with his removal from normal duties and assign-

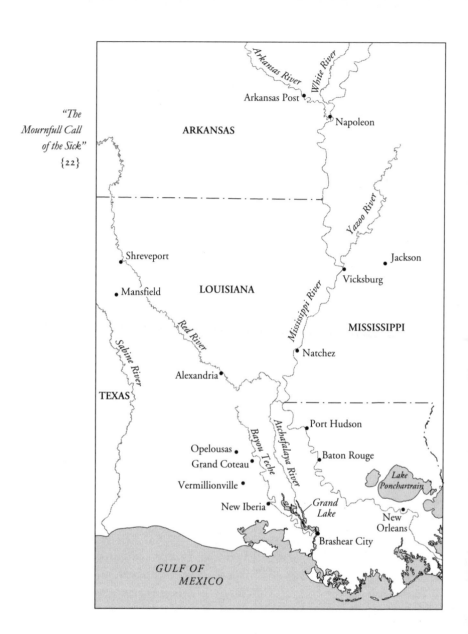

The lower Mississippi Valley

ment to the hospital. He seems also to have been a good and consci-
entious nurse, however, and that too may have influenced his supe-
riors to retain him on medical duty, for such traits were not necessarily
typical of Civil War male nurses. Back home, caring for the sick was
mostly women's work. Historian Reid Mitchell has commented on the
efforts of Civil War soldiers to fill in their all-male camps some of the
roles that women had usually filled in their families before the war.[1]

Once again Winters's mention of his children is revealing. A friend
had related in a letter to him what his daughter Edith had said about
his absence. Edith was less inclined than her mother to put on a
brave front and had confessed that both her mother and her younger
brother, Willie, spent a good deal of time crying over William's absence. Young Edith Winters's stake in the war was simple and enor-
mous: "She wanted [Northern forces] to whip the rebels so that [her
father] could come home." This touching glimpse into the Winters
household shows us a warm, close family with a father who must have
been involved enough with his children for them all, from youngest to
oldest, to feel his absence intensely and painfully.

Duty in the field hospital brought less fatigue and exposure than
that with the regiment but also far more opportunity to witness the
suffering and death of other soldiers. Death must have seemed all
around him and even where he had least expected it. His diary and
letters during this period reflect the hardships that tested the fortitude
of soldiers off the battlefield as much and perhaps more than in
action. As one Civil War officer put it, "A soldier is not a hero in
fighting alone; his patience under hardship, privation and sickness is
equally heroic; sometimes I feel disposed to put him on a level with
the martyrs."[2]

Yet even in the midst of these difficult circumstances—and maybe
because of them—William Winters was quick to notice the beauties
and curiosities of the land around him. As spring began to crowd out
the long and dismal winter, Winters wished he could send his wife "a
nice beauquet [bouquet] of spring flowers such as roses, dafodils,
pinks, violits, snow drops." They were "all in full bloom," he informed
her, "and the woods, fields, and heges are puting on their sumer cloth-

ing." It was enough to make a stolid Hoosier downright lyrical: "The morning air smells sweet with the perfume of wild flowers and sings with the merey song of mocking bird and robin." Yet the shadow of war was ever present. "Were it not for the incesant rattle of drums and fifes in the diferent regiments," Winters wrote, "I would never supose that war was in the land, only from the desolation that it leaves behind."

⌒🐃

Thursday, [January] 22, [1863]
Today we have done nothing. lost another man today. makes four since we left Mem[phis].

Friday, [January] 23, [1863]
Ordered to go ashore & have the quarters all cleaned up. got out & was ordered back again. droped down the river a mile or so & the boys packed up, got everything of[f] the boat & set around until dark & came aboard for the night. raining.

Saturday, [January] 24, [1863]
Coughed all night last night & got no sleep at all for it. received two letters yesterday, one from my wife & one from Lavinea. Jo Carmichael arrived here yesterday with a couple of the boys from home. Jo got wounded in the shoulder on the way down here by guerillas firing into the boat & wounded several.[3] we put quite a number of the 67 on board the Fanny Bullitt[4] to go to the general hospital. the boys are all gone to camp some five miles from the boat. I have just finished writing to my wife. [Letter not found.]

[The first page of this letter is missing, but the content identifies it as having been written from the vicinity of Vicksburg, January 24, 1863.]
it is a bad wet drearey night, and I expect that the boys are in a bad fix at camp, as I dont think that they got to camp in time to make themselves comfortable before night, and the ground is wet and muddy.
we are waiting for the river to rise more and for grants forces to

join us here before making the atack on Vicksburgh. the rebels are making a great blow about the men that left the fleet to be paroled on our way down here. they say that our armey is intirely demoralised and that our men are diserting every day and going over to them to be paroled to get out of the fighting to free the negroes; and I expect that some of them have told the rebbels that kind of a story, no doubt, but they will find out when we go at them again how bad of[f] we are, as the detirmanation is to take Vicksburgh at all hazards.

Cap[tain] Eaton and lieut Akin are both sick yet but have both gone to camp with the regiment, I believe.[5] wes left us for home on last Sunday on bord the tow boat Luzurn for Memphis and will probably get there before you get this, and he can tell you more about the fight at Arkansas Post than I can write and give you a history of our trip up and down the Mississippi. it will be interesting and amusing, some parts of it. Jo Gambold gave me a letter to read that Philip wrote to him some time ago. he said that Edith had just been in the shop after some shaveings and she said her ma had got a letter from her pa, and that she wanted us to whip the rebels so that I could come home; that ma always cryed when she got a letter from her pa and willey was always calling for me, and she wanted me to come home again. I wish I was there to night with you insted of here writeing to you and listening for the mournfull call of the sick, for I am tired and wearey watching twelve hours a day from noon untill midnight. we have lost four men on our trip from death out of the regiment since we left Memphis.

I got a letter from Lavina on yesterday, and I will enclose it with this to you, and you can see her card she sent me. if wes is at home I want him to write what company orlando is lieut in, as I want to write to him. I must write to vine as she was verey anxious to hear from me.

well, I have just got some water for some of the sick and smoothed down their pallets of blankets and must hurrey and finish before midnight, as I want to sleep some to night, as I slept none last night at all for my cough. you need not be uneasy about me as I will get along, I guess, without any trouble. if I could be at home to night to get a good slice of your bread and butter, I would give a great deal. we can get butter here for fifty cts a pound, but I have no money atall. you must excuse me for not paying the postage. it is getting late, and I must stop at this. hat, if you only knew how I long to se[e] you and my litle ones, you would know how I loved you all and longed to be at home. kiss them for me and write as often as you can.

Wm. Winters

give my love to all and tell them to write and I will answer as soon as posible. my love to all. good night. Bill.

Sunday, [January] 25, [1863]

Today we finished putting of our sick on board the J. E. Swan.[6] we removed the sick of several other regiments besides our own & now we are waiting for orders. the report is tonight that the rebels are agoing to try to take the whole fleet, as several rebel rams have been seen on the Yazoo river today. One of our gunboats run & captured a rebel transport loaded with troops rasing from Vicksburgh. we also took some prisoners besides. am on the Fanny Bullitt—our doctors are in charge of the boat.

Monday, [January] 26, [1863]

Been busy all day. have been four deaths on board since I came on board. had a little good luck last night when the details were made. I had the luck to be extra & got a good nights sleep by it.

Tuesday, [January] 27, [1863]

There was another death aboard last night. the sick complain of not getting enough to eat—the nurses do. we have had another death today. it is quite cold & chilly today for this climate & the sick feel it more so. worked hard today on account of the cold.

Wednesday, [January] 28, [1863]

Today there has been four deaths in the different wards. I have had but one in my ward as yet. been very busy—have had no relief for 38 hours. saw some of the boys from the regiment today. they are faring better than we are. Jo Carmichael & Eli Zigler[7] came on board today.

Thursday, [January] 29, [1863]

Today has been about as the proceeding one. we lost three more men today by deaths, one from my ward. it froze yesterday in the shade all day. we had a lot more sick put on bord today.

Friday, [January] 30, [1863]

Today it has been the same old routine of duties as usual. we have had three more deaths on board today, one in my ward.

Saturday, [January] 31, [1863]

Today we left our landing & ran up the river about twenty five miles for wood in company with 9 other boats, to be gone two or three days. the captain of this boat says that he is ordered to report back again untill the men are paid off.

February, Sunday, 1st, [1863]

Today is the first of the week & the first of the month, but it has no appearance of Sunday at all. we have been wooding all day long— tonight we go up the river a little farther for more wood. we buried three more dead that died today.

Monday, [February] 2, [1863]

Today we have finished wooding & the duties have been the same as usual. we lost two more by death today. we have heard heavy cannonading today all day in the direction of the Yazoo river.[8]

Tuesday, [February] 3, [1863]

This morning took on a few more cords wood & ran down to our old landing in the fleet. we buried two more men before we left this morning. two of our gunboats run the blockade on yesterday which was the cause of the firing we heard.[9]

Wednesday, [February] 4, [1863]

Went out to the regiment this morning. saw all the boys. some have the chills & a good many the diareah & none of them seemed to be in very good spirits. camp is in a rather bad place as are all the rest. it has been raining nearly all day hard—had to move some of our sick to-night out of the wet as the roof leaks bad in some places.

Thursday, [February] 5, [1863]
Today has been one of the most fatal since I have been on board the Bullitt. there have been 8 deaths in the different wards today. this morning we dropped down the river some 3 or 4 miles to take on coal & we are now in plain view of a portion of the rebel works back of Vicksburgh. we can plainly see a very large rebel flag flying from one of their forts.

Friday, [February] 6, [1863]
Today we have been very busy all day getting our sick ready for the city of Memphis. 4 deaths.

Saturday, [February] 7, [1863]
Slept all the forenoon today. work hard all the afternoon removing the sick. Got them all off after dark awhile. Three died during the removal.

Sunday, [February] 8, [1863]
Slept all night last night for the first time in several weeks. Been busy all day cleaning up.

Monday, [February] 9, [1863]
Finished cleaning up today—worked very hard & at nasty work.

Tuesday, [February] 10, [1863]
Today we finished the work on board & took our depart for camp. got out about suppertime. surprised all the boys. they thought I had gone up the river.

Wednesday, [February] 11, [1863]
Today have rested all day. I am quite sick. the boys are all down in spirits.

Thursday, [February] 12, [1863]

Today I am about as I was yesterday. the company are out on picket today. wrote to my [wife] today. [Letter not found.]

Friday, [February] 13, [1863]

Today I went back into the hospital. I am not able for duty, but they want me in preferance. found things in a rather bad fix—cleaned up as well as I could.

Saturday, [February] 14, [1863]

This morning the Brigade are under marching orders & the boys are all in a hurry cooking rations & getting [illegible]. destination unknown. well, the boys have just left for up the river on a scout.

Sunday, [February] 15, [1863]

It has rained nearly all night last night with very severe thunder & lighting, & it looks still like raining, & it is muddy & slop[p]y getting around. two more gunboats run the blockade night before last.[10]

Monday, [February] 16, [1863]

It is still raining today all day—rained nearly all night. one of our Company died last night, the first we have lost since we have been in the service. he is a married man from Hartsville, James Mobley.[11] Tonight we have our hospital full on account of the rain, as it is still pouring down.

Tuesday, [February] 17, [1863]

Raining still. went down to the bakers this morning after bread for the hospital & liked to have got a horse fast in the mud but didn't. never saw so mutch mud & water in may life. everything is mud, and still it gets muddier still.

Wednesday, [February] 18, [1863]

This morning when I first got up it was drisiling yet, but it has finealy held up for a while. there are some heavy guns being fired in the direction of Vicksburgh—don't know what it all means.[12]

Thursday, [February] 19, [1863]

This morning I am extremely sore & my kidneys hurt me very mutch. the sun is shining out today & the prospects look good for fair weather for a while. sun red tonight—fair day tomorrow.

Friday, [February] 20, [1863]

It is a beautiful day—things around camp look more cheerfull, & the sick are in mutch better spirits. there has been but little of interest today.

Saturday, [February] 21, [1863]

It is raining again as usual. heard today that our whole brigade has been captured again somewhere in the neighborhood of Arkansas river—don't believe it.[13] nothing of interest today.

Sunday, [February] 22, [1863]

This is Washington's birthday & the aniversary of the Battle of Monterey,[14] & it is a passibly fair day. Heard today that the rebels captured our ram that run the blockade a short time ago. There was some tremendous heavy firing night before last but don't believe that was the cause of it.[15] Perminas Lick died today about 10 o'clock. he did not know he was dieing.[16]

Monday, [February] 23, [1863]

I received a letter from home on yesterday with the sad intelligence that one of my children was dead & my wife is very sick. We had nothing of note in camp today.

in Camp near Youngs Point, L.A.

Feb. 23rd, 1863

Dear wife, it is with feelings of the deepest grief that I attempt to answer your last that I received yesterday afternoon with the sad news of our little willie['s] death and your illness. it would have been hard enough to give him up if I had been at hom[e], but to me it was doubley so. to only think that I could not even see his little face once more or hear his inocent pratle again is enough to make me wis[h] that I had never left you or them but let the government taken care of itself, but an alwise [all-wise] providence has ruled otherwise, and it is for us to bear the stroke, hard as it is to bear, but I hope that you are entirely well, but I fear you did not write how bad you was, fearing to write to[o] mutch sad news at one time, but I hope that you and our two little girls are all out of danger. if I had known that you were all sick, I would have tryed to come home at some cost or other, but I didnot know anything about you and willies being sick untill I received the sad news that he was dead. oh how I wish that this dreadfull war was over and I had the pleasure of seeing the remainder of my family, for it is to[o] late to wish to see Will, but I hope that my life may be spared to meet you all again.

I had just finished the last kind offices of friendship for Permenas Lick. I gave him his last dose of medicine and the last drink of water that he took on earth and closed his eyes in death. I nursed him for about a week or a little over and done all in my power, but it was of no avail. he sank gradualey down untill he died, which was as calm and quiet as if he had been going to sleep. Cap[tain] Eaton has sent some of the men down to one of the boats for a coffin for him, and we will burie him this afternoon. he died about two oclock yesterday. if you se[e] his mother tell her he died as he had lived, a good boy.[17] I must close as the mail is about to leave.

good by. I am well. write soon.

Tuesday, [February] 24, [1863]

Today it is quite warm & drying very fast. there is some fireing going on in the direction of Vicksburgh—don't know the cause. we have had five deaths in the hospital since I came to the Reg[iment].[18]

Wednesday, [February] 25, [1863]

It is about two oclock in the morning, & I have been listening at the rebels fireing at some of our gunboats runing the blockade. they let go some big ones. the first one down gave them a broadside as she passed, but the second one took no notice of them at all but to blow her whistle, a signal that she was all right.[19]

Thursday, [February] 26, [1863]

It has rained all night, & it looks gloomy enough. I think it rained as hard as I ever saw it, & it still continues to rain. the brigade has just returned—13 days out. the boys say they had some fine times eating honey, molasses, chickens, etc.[20] the hospital is full again. a good many cases came in with the Reg[iment], some very bad ones. the boys captured horses, mules, 60 hogs, chickens, ducks, hams & shoulders, yams, & whatever they could find to eat.

Friday, [February] 27, [1863]

It is pleasant today again. heard that the rebels had taken our gunboat Indianola but dont know how it is. Camp [illegible] are rather scarce, the printer not having time to get his forms up since the boys came back.

Saturday, [February] 28, [1863]

Made some changes in our hospital arrangements. Captn Eaton received a box of things his wife sent to him. they were nearly all spoiled. we have all mustered for pay today. dont know when we will get it.

Sunday, [March] 1st, [1863]

It is fair & butifull today. heard part of a funeral sermon preached over two soldiers today, the first thing of the kind I have heard in the army. it sound solemn. wrote a letter to my wife today. there is a flag of truce in just now but learn its meaning or from which side it is from. the rebels sent it to confer about forageing.

Camp, Youngs Point, L.A., March 1st, [18]63

Dear wife, it is sunday morning and a verey pleasant morning and being off from duty untill noon I thought that I would write again without waiting for an answer to my last, hopeing that you and the children have entirely recovered. I have been verey uneasey about you since I heard that you was not able to go to willies funeral for fear you did not tell me how sick you was. I was fearfull from the first I heard of willies being sick, that he would not get well. I dont know why it was, but I could not help thinking that I would hear bad news from home, and I have the same fears yet that I havent heard it all. now I want you to write imeaditly [immediately] and let me know the worst and how bad it is.

the wether has been verey wet and disagreeable for the most of the time that we have been here and the health of the army does not improve. Garrett DeGarmo[21] is quite sick, and a boy by the name of Burchfield[22] from Hartsville is verey sick and there are several others that are unfit for duty. Cap[tain] Eaton received a box of things from his wife but they had been on the road so long that the most of the things were entirely spoiled. Clint Naleys[23] things that were sent in it from his fathers wedding were in a bad fix. his gum drops were all disolved and his loaf suger was tainted so by the other things spilling on it that it was not fit to eat. it is to[o] far to try to send anything down here as it takes to[o] long to come.

I would like verey mutch to be at home this morning to see you all and get a dinner that was cooked once more, but that is denied me and I must be content with what we have.

The boys have got back from their scout up the river. instead of being gone seven days, they were gone thirteen. the boys I guess enjoyed it pretty well, as the[y] were alowed to forage a goodeal [good deal], and they mad[e] good use of the privelage, as they got pleanty of chickens, ducks, sweet potatoes, hams, eggs, and honey, to say nothing of fresh pork, beef, and corn bread, butter, and milk. there is some talk of sending them out again, and the boys all seem to be anxious to go. gen Burbrige[24] is trying to have them all mounted so as to chase guerilas succesfully, as they could have captured a lot on the other scout with a battrey of six guns if they could have traveled fast enough to, but the rebels were to[o] fast, all being mounted, and infantry couldnt overtake them. the[y] got some thirty prisoners and diserters and one twelve-pound gun that they [the Confederates] left in their hurey to get away. they brought back a good maney milk cows and cattle besides mules and horses.

we were all mustered for pay on yesterday. I only lack five days of being two months in the hospital. The extra pay makes the wages 20 dollars and 50 cents a month, which is better than 13, I think, and thus it is not quite so hard sometimes, and the pay is what I want.[25] we received two mails this week, and I expected an answer from wes, but it came not to hand now. I want wes to tell me what the prospects are and how the people are taking the afair, as we hear all kinds of rumors and reports about what the folks are doeing at home and what the democrats are trying to do. I want you to tell me if you have to move or not, and I want wes to tell Jerey George I think he is not to be dependid upon or he would have made you that deed. I want wes to make him come to terms.

it is getting to be nearly dinner time and I have to go on duty at twelve oclock. I hope that this will find you and my two little pets well.

Tell them that pa thinks about them and wishes maney a time that he could kiss them before he goes to bed. How often I sit in the sick room at midnight with no company but the sick and no sound but the groans and inchoherant muterings of the feaver racked brain of some poor mortal as he begs for his wife and little ones or asks for his mother to come and take him home, and often as I sit and listen I think of my own home and my wife and children and shead tears of sorow at the thought of our being so far apart that either might die and the other know nothing of it for weeks after, perhaps as it was when poor willie died, but I sincerly hope that I may be permited to get home again safe. give my love to all and tell them to write and I will answer. write soon.

Wm. Winters to my wife

Monday, [March] 2, [1863]
Nothing of interest today that I have heard of only the report that our brigade is to be stationed at Greenville.

Tuesday, [March] 3, [1863]
All the same old biz over today only the rebels tried their hand at shelling our forces at work on the cut off, doing no damage.[26] the boys got marching orders again with tenn days rations—destination unknown, but it is a scout up the river somewhere.

Wednesday, [March] 4, [1863]

The boys are off once more, all that are able to go. we have been trying a couple of 20 lb. parots at a target this afternoon. got a letter from C. S. Bointon[27] with the present of a memorandum book & gave my mind relief concerning my family. we have finealy got our sick all on cots, & the rooms look comfortable.

Thursday, [March] 5, [1863]

It cool & chilley this morning & I am about half sick but have to go through at some rate or other. got relieve for the night.

Friday, [March] 6, [1863]

Answered Dr. Bointon letter today. received orders to send our sick on board hospital boat. I hope they will send all as I think they ought to go up the river.

Saturday, [March] 7, [1863]

Put nearly all our sick on board hospital boat City of Memphis[28] today. Many of them will never see home again—some begged not to be sent away among strangers. heard nothing of any note today more than the report is the sick are all being sent away in anticipation of an attack on Vicksburgh in short time.[29]

Sunday, [March] 8, [1863]

Well, a great many of the troops will remember [this day] on acount of having to skedadle from their quarters in double guick, the leavy [levy] breaking just below them. they had to travel, the water raising five feet in twenty four hours where it was dry the day before. our brigade got back again today haveing foraged five days. the boys brought back plenty of fowls, yams, molasses, etc.

Monday, [March] 9, [1863]

Troops moving out of the way of the water all day. expect we will have to go tomorrow. there has been some heavy fireing today up the Yazoo river & from the point above Vicksburgh. I understand it is signal fireing from our fleet. the report is that we have taken Yazoo city & that Grant's forces are above the bluffs on the Yazoo river.[30]

Tuesday, [March] 10, [1863]

Got orders to strike tents & be ready to move at one oclock. got everything packed & embarked on board the Maria Dunning.[31] Piled down on some tents for the night. waked up in the night; found it raining hard & leaking on me. had to spread my oil blanket over me to keep dry. waked up at Milicans bend. got off at Millican town—got a house for our hospital & fixed up in a very pleasant place.

Wednesday, [March] 11, [1863]

Took a stroll around town this morning. found the boys cooking breakfast in the mud. some of the company here & some of them having quartered themselves as best they could around in houses, stables, & sheds. saw quite a number of houses that had the marks of canon balls through them. the building our hospital is in has a couple through it. the boys go into camp here today. it rained terribly last night & the ground is mudy for shure.

Thursday, [March] 12, [1863]

I took a walk around a small grave yard this morning for my morning walk just below here. it has some very good work in it. three or four monuments or tombs, one with a lamb on the head of it in the act of getting up off from a rockey ground work. the foundation is here in one corner of the yard. the parsonage the men here of the diferant reg[iments] have entirely ruined.

Friday, [March] 13, [1863]

Took a stroll down to the reg[iment] this morning. the first time I have been down to the boys new quarters. found them all busily engaged reading letters & papers from home. news all good. got a letter from my wife. family all well. the ground where the reg[iment] is encamped is wet, mudy, & mirey from appearances. heard from H. F. Claude & the other boys that went in with him. they are all at St. Louis,

Mo., cor[ner] 5th & Chestnut street[s]. Harey is down with the in-
flamatory rhuematism.

saw a runaway [horse] this morning and upset & a spill out in front
of the shack of an old irish woman & her little boys. two boats come
up last night with troops from below. saw something that I never saw
before today & yesterday & that was pumkins from last year sound &
good as when they first came of[f] the vines.

Saturday, [March] 14, [1863]
Things are about as usual as far as I have heard. answered my wife's
letter this morning. had to report to the colonel—did so & was ordered back to the hospital again for duty all night.

Sunday, [March] 15, [1863]
Sabath morning & a raining with a gloomy apearance. the day
pegged off as it comenced—wet.

Monday, [March] 16, [1863]
This morning the fog is almost so dense that you may feel it but not
quite—cleard of[f] so as we could heer fireing in the direction of
Vicksburgh from our mortors. some of the heavyest fireing that has
been done was after dark last night.[32]

Tuesday, [March] 17, [1863]
Took a walk out the road to the picket line this morning to look at
the country & to see Co. I. they being on picket duty. saw some nice
catfish the boys had caught in the bayou close by. there is quite a
number of boats loaded with troops going up the river, destination
unknown. rumor says we go to Helena [Arkansas] in a short time to
relieve some of Grants men.

Wednesday, [March] 18, [1863]
Hear a big report last night to the effect that some of our forces &
gunboats had got through the Yazoo pass at friars point to Yazoo
river & drove the rebel gunboats & transports down towards our fleet

below & they took refuge in a bayou & we captured the whole lot, 6,000, & 75 gun & transport boats, but I think it is to[o] good to be true.[33]

sent of[f] a case of varioloid this morning—expect small pox next in order.[34]

weather very fine. several boats passed down this evening, one gunboat with dispatches. I guess there was a mail today, but I got no letters or papers.

Thursday, [March] 19, [1863]

There has been very heavy firing all night making the earth hereabouts tremble.[35] the regiment has just drawn a lot of clothing for the boys. some more boats down this morning. I hope they have brought late news for me. some of the regiment are being paid off here now. I hope our turn will come soon.

Friday, [March] 20, [1863]

The morning is as fair as needs be & the roar of artilery that has been at work at intervals all night is no longer to be heard. had a general clean up in the wards today. the medical inspector is making his anual rounds & we must of needs look neat & clean. got a letter from my wife today with one enclosed from R. E. S. All well excepting Wesley. our teamsters & cavalry have been bringing in a vast amount of cotton, corn, & forage from the country.

Saturday, [March] 21, [1863]

Well, we are trying to finish cleaning up today. the Brigade is ordered to be ready to move at any time at an hours warning. heard a report that Gen. Gorman had taken hainses bluf & held it but cant say how true it is, but I think it is corect. there has been heavy canonading in that direction for a couple of days. the fireing from the direction of Vicksburgh last night was terible. the flashes of the guns were plainly visable here resembling the flashes of heat lightning on a sumers evening & the reports were like some terible thunder shakeing the earth here untill the glass in the windows & the botles in the hospital ratled & clinged again.[36]

᠅

The following letter was written to Winters by a "Mrs. Wooden," the sister of Pvt. Parmenias H. Lick, who died under Winters's care on February 22, 1863. Mrs. Wooden's spelling and punctuation are similar in quality to Winters's, and all punctuation has been added by the editor. The letter is a clear illustration of nineteenth-century ideas about dying.

᠅

St. Louis Crossing
March the 21st, 1863

Mr. Winters, kind sir

I, to satisfy a troubled and anxious mind, set myself down an take the libberty to address you. although I do not know you personaly, yet I learned from different sources that you was the kind nurse of my Brother *Permenas H. Lick.* He stated in his last letters which he ever wrote that "he had Mr. Winters for his nurs, an as good a nurse as ever was, that you did evry thing in your power for him, an for us not to be uneasy about him." this was only four days before his death. For this kindness toward my dear Brother I canot express my deep feelings of gratitude towards you.

We all join in expressions of thanks to you for the favors Our dear Brother recived from you hands. We also join in tendering our heart felt thanks to Capt Eaton for his kindness toward him an also for his kindness in writing so soon an writeing to my only Brother so soon which we think shows a very humane heart also a very sympathetic one. we[']re thankful that he was burried with as much respect as he was by his captian an nurse. It is a fixed principle with us all to pray for soldiers, But be assured that through strong feelings of gratitude and affection to you and your kind Captain (a Captian any Soldier shoud love an be proud of) our prayrs ascend day and night to God to preserve your lives and health and Charicters and that He may shield you in the [h]our of battle and if you should have to lye in Hospital sick, O, may you have some kind hand to administer to you wants, and if you should die in an enimys land m[a]y you die a Christian as did my Brother. But I pray God to spare your lives evry one of you, to see rebellion so crushed that it shall not be able to raise its hienous form again neither south or north and evry traitor and rebel shall share rebel doom. Now, kind sir, as I remarked in the onset, to ease a troubled mind I wis[h] you, if you please, to write to me and let me have all the particulars of my dear Brothers illness and death. I know he always was a good boy, has been a member of the Church six years and one month to the very day he died, was truely converted. he wrote home several times about his serious feelings and his secret prayrs and reading his bible. But his death was so suden I want to know what you think could have been the matter. in his letter just four days before his death, he says he was well with the exception of strength. had he a sergion, a physician, that knew anything? what was his name? how often did he see him? did he do his duty by him and tell him he could not get well? do you think that Brother thought at anytime he had to die? if he did, what did he say in reference to death? was he willing and ready or was he snatched of[f] without knowing any thing about it? I wish to know how it was exactly—just what he said. what were his last word or words? did he wish to be at home? did he wish to see mother or any one else? was he in his right mind? did he pray any? did he make any request about his burrial or his grave? did he wish to be sent right home? did he say anything about his cloths, what should be done with them, his keepsakes, or any request any way? what cloths did [he] die in, and what did you burey him? was it a white shirt?

The remainder of this sad letter is missing. In an April 14 letter to his wife, Winters noted receiving this letter, expressed his intention of answering it that evening, and stated that he would enclose Mrs. Wooden's letter with the one to his wife. Apparently he did, and that explains our possession of at least this much of it today.

Milicans Stores,[37] Loisana, March 21st, 1863

Dear wife, it is with mutch pleasure that I answer yours of the 7th for by it I found that you had entirely recovered and that the children are both well. we are enjoying the finest of spring weather, and I would give a goodeal [good deal] if I could send you a nice beauquet [bouquet] of spring flowers such as roses, dafodils, pinks, violits, snow drops, and most of the other kinds that I dont know the names of, as they are all in full bloom, and the woods, fields, and heges are puting on their sumer clothing, and during the day it makes me feel as if I would like to put mine on, if I had aney. the morning air smells sweet with the perfume of wild flowers and sings with the merey song of mocking bird and robin and were it not for the incesant rattle of drums and fifes in the diferent regiments, I would never supose that war was in the land, only from the desolation that it leaves behind.

for let me give you a little idea of the destruction of property. here was a place about half as big as Hope and with some verey fine dwelings in it, but, alas, where are they now? not one of them is left, only the few that are ocupied as hospitals and generals headquarters, and they are all damaged more or less. when the division come here, it was verey wet and mudey, and the boys had to have floores in their tents to keep them from mireing down, and the consequence is that every fence mad[e] of planks and the houses were torn down to make floors and tables, and now you cant see fence or rail as far as your eyes can reach but what is used or burned. the teams go out into the country for 2 and 3 miles and haul in rails for fire wood, and the country begins to look desolate enough, but what it will look like if we stay here a month or two nobody can tell. a rebel came into camp the other day and asked the permision of general Smith[38] if he might raise a crop out here about 10 miles, and the gen told him he might but he must not gather it after he had raised it, as he [Smith] must have all that was raised for the men under his command, and the felow left, I guess thinking that he had better go home and move further back or he could not plant any thing this sumer.

the river is verey high yet, and it makes it rather worse camping, as the surface of the water in the river is some three feet higher than the surface of the ground is where we are all encamped. we have got a verey nice house for our hospital and pleanty of shade around it, fig trees in the garden and china trees in the front and both side gardens. it is a pity to se[e] how some butifull yards and houses are distroyed. the cavalry and teamsters are forageing all the time, bringing in all the cattle, hogs, horses, sheep, mules, and chickens, in fact, everything that they can use at all they take from the rebels. we have been liveing high here, for some times between what we draw from our ration and what we capture from the rebels and sanitary stores that are sent down the river for the hopsitals. we have had a fat time for awhile, but how long it will last is the question. we have fresh beaf, fresh pork, chickens, buter, molases, onions, potatoes, pickels, dried aples, and peaches and apple butter, besides some green apples—all sanitary goods sent down for the use of the hospitals.[39] we have 22 sick in our hospital at present with some more that ought to be here, but we havent got room for them. [Would] you please tell dock [Doctor] Stapp that Bill everoade[40] is down at youngs point, down sick with the small pox, but he is getting some better. the columbus[41] company have 3 cases of small pox and two cases of varioloid. they are all down at the point, I belive, in a general hospital. we have had one case of varioloid here in the hospital, but that is all, but the small pox is spreading, and I expect we will have an awful time here yet. you need not tell any body but Stapp, as it would make a great many uneasy. the doctors have been vacinating for some time as fast as they could to check the disease before it gets started. if you see B Maddy's[42] wife, tell her he is better & that he is up and about, helping us clean up the hospital for general inspection tomorow. Elijah dudly is here very sick.[43] Jim Israel, Charly Cook, and Lewis Hegecock are all three discharged from the service for inability to perform active duty.[44] Garret DeGarmo[45] is up the river somewhere sick, but I dont know where. we havent heard from him since he left camp. our brigade is ordered to hold itself in readiness to march at an hours notice and every thing is bustle and confusion. expecting the order every day. we may be here when you get this, and we may be in vicksburgh, and we may not, but I think that the fate of vicksburgh or of this army will be told before this gets to you, but I cant say, but this I know: the trial is at hand. I have saw four battle fields and god knows that I dont want to se[e] another, but I expect to and that before ten days are gone. some of company I, 67[th], have writen nearly their last letter home, but who it is no one can tell yet.

give my best love and respects to all enquiring friends and tell them to keep traitors straight at home and we will atend to these down here. I will write again before we move if we have to take our sick with us; if we dont I will stay here. I am well and hope that this will find you all the same. [no signature]

Sunday, [March] 22, [1863]

Well, we have got our hospital all cleaned up & everything in order ready for the coming of the great inspector general of the medical department. the day is a butiful one with a nice cool balmy brease blowing. the cavalry escort to the wagon train is all ready for the country as they go out today for cotton & forage the same as any other day. 30 teams have just passed. I counted 25 loads of cotton on yesterday besides the fodder, rails, & other stuf thats being hauled in all day. the report is here today that Farigut is at the mouth of the canal below Vicksburgh & that is where the heavy fireing is from that we heard last night & the night before.[46] Cap[tain] Eaton has finaly got Jim Israel, Charley Cook, & Clint Nealey[47] discharged & the best of it is he has got his own in the bargain. We have two of the most trouble-some cases in the hospital now that I have ever saw—Geo. Oldham & Henry Doan.[48] they beat all, as frank says.

Monday, [March] 23, [1863]

Raining to kep its hand in, I guess. rained all night last night & bids fair to make a rainy day of it today. there was five cavalry boats come down the river yesterday & two rams. I heard this morning that they brought a heavy mail for the army here. I hope I have a share in the pile from home. the packet Omaha just passed down. the names of the cavalry boats are Autocrat, Adams, Baltic, Diana, & E. N. Fair-child.[49] heard some of the heaviest fireing done today about 10 oclock that I have ever heard & the fastest for heavy guns.[50] two mails down but I got nothing—cant account for it.

Camp, April 2, Millicans Stores, 1863

Dear wife, I received yours and wesleys of March the 15th and was glad to hear that you were all well. I read a letter yesterday that Fred Bannes[51] got from his beloved Mary and got me to answer. she wrote that John Gambold was dead. I was quite astonished to hear that he had died, as thought that John would get well enough to get home.[52] I knew that he would never be of any service to the government again, but I thought that he would get a discharge and live perhaps a year, but John Burcham, I expected to hear of his death, so it did not surprise me to hear that he was dead.[53] I will tell you what suppriesed and disgusted all the boys here more than any thing that we have all heard since we left home, and that was Joe Burchams marriage. the boys down here all think that he had better have waited untill his first wife was buried before he commenced courting his second. the boys have all set him down a peg lower in their estimation.

well, Hat, I expect that [you'll] have had the pleasure of Capt Eaton and ladies campany before you get this. I sent you two letters by him. one was on some leaves of a little Blank Book and I hadnt the time to get an envelope for it before he left, but there is nothing in it if he should take the liberty to read it, as I hadnt the time to finish it and [he] promised to take his lady and spend the evening with you as soon as he got home. he was the gladest man to get a discharge that I have seen for some time now I asure you.[54] well, I hope that old Mrs Hedgecock has seen her son Lewis, for he is a promising lad. I think if he has no bad luck he will seed the whole family comfortubley with both head and body lice, so you can be a little careful of them, espe-cially if you see them rubing first here and then there, as he was to[o] lazy here to enjoy good health, for he would lay in the tent, his mess would get breakfast, and then he would get up, eat as mutch as he could hold, and then lay down again and feel for lice.[55] I think from what I have seen of him that the whole family will do to keep clear of. Rhodies delectable sugar lump, Anderson Read, is about dito, and they ought to all be pend up together.[56]

I was agoing to send you up a little box of rebel flower plants by the capt, but he was not well, and the boys that come home with [him] were no better than he was, and I thought that it would perhaps cost you a dollar, and [I] knew that you had no money to pay for flowers, and I didn't dig them. if we are ordered up to Kentucky pretty soon, as I think we will be, and we ever get paid off again, I will try to send you up some, especially some Blackberrys there are down here in a garden that have a double flower. I will send two or three of these flowers up in this letter and you can se[e] the[y] look verey mutch like a small white rose. I wish that this cursed rebelion would stop while we are down here, and I would then pack a box full of roots and plants and bring them home with me, but I guess it never will be ended unless the armies are doing more at other places than they are here since we have been down in the neighborhood of Vicksburgh, for there is more men here than I ever saw before. the whole country is being covered with tents as they arive and go into camp, brigade after brigade. General Curtises[57] whole armey is to be here, I believe. Major General Hamiltons division of it is all ready here, and the balance is to be here this week, I believe.[58]

well, Hat, it['s] almost daylight and I must stop for to night. a squad of cavalry scouts are just passing [the] window and I can see the form of one rebel prisoner. goodnight.

well, Hat, it['s] my watch again and I will take advantage of the idle moments to fill this sheet of paper for you. I have had the painfull duty of helping to lay out two men that have died since I finished writing this morning and expect to have the same painfull duty to perform on two or three more before tomorrow morning, all typhoid fever case[s]. it is feerfully fatal down here on our men. unless a case can be taken out of the tents and atended to constantly, the case is hopeless, as they soon get beyond doing anything for them atall. in some cases in 24 hours they cant take a few drops of water from a spoon even. one poor fellow we could do nothing for atall. after he came into the hospital, he lay and screamed untill he died, about two days. I saw Ed Gorden and Elij McGlocklin on yesterday. they were both well. Elij said that I should tell wes that he weighed 15 pounds more now than he ever did in his life. his cheeks stick out like a china pigs. pino and him are both on guard at McClernods Head quarters. Elij says they live fat and have a fine time.

the officer of the day has just been in making his daily round of inspection to se[e] if everything was all clean and neat. complimented old Davenport[59] and myself and went about his business allright. it is a butifull day to[day]. the sun shines out hot, and the birds sing merily from every bush and twig, and I almost forget sometimes that I am in an enemys country as I sit museing at the windows on the lavished buties of nature spread out before me as far as the eye can reach on either hand. every thing is green here now and looks like summer already.

I have to jump up so often to keep a boy on his cot that is lying here at my left hand that I forget my train of thought. well, it is very near night again and I will have to finish this to night. I washed me a pair of pants and a shirt and pair of socks this forenoon. now I have all of my clothes clean again.

half past one oclock on my morning watch and I have just helped to carry out of the room another of earths inhabitants that is no more for ever.

it is a butifull night, Hat, and the moon that is shining on us so splendidly is shining on our home and loved ones, but, oh, its shining on two diferant elements. here is a mighty army dressed in panolply of war, and there is the abode of peace and loves home ties, all that the soldier longs for. but here we are, and I guess the fates have decreed that we shall stay here or some where else but not go home. no, that would not do.

well, Hat, it is getting towards the close of this sheet of paper, and I will have to soon say my say out for tonight. I wish I could peep in and see you and the children and see how you spend your evenings and hear their innocent prattle about the rebels and what they are agoing to do when pa comes home. the time I hope will come after awhile when we can all come together on a triumphal march home with peace in all the world. I hope that some of those infernal whelps there at home that are doing all they dare will have to come down here, and I know some of them will get the conceit taken out as there is some lead waiting for them here the first little fray that comes off, for there is more than one man swore he would shoot so and so, if he could get him down here, for sentiments he has uttered since this last freak of theirs.[60] so the boys talk from diferant places.

well, I want you to tell Edith and Mary [May] that they must hurry and learn to write to pa, as he wants to hear from them both. tell them to be good girls and maybe pa will get home by and by. kiss them both for me. give all my friends my best respects and write what kind of a time they had when Lewis got home. From Your afectionate Husband Wm. Winters

tell vin and mollie I will write them both a letter next week. I have a couple of men picked out for them. Bill.

Millicans Stores, L.A., April 7, 1863

Dear wife, it is with more than usual pleasure that I sit down to write to you this morning, for I feel more than well, as we have actually been paid off, as you will see by the contents of this and the way in which it is sent. I enclose you fifty dollars hopeing that it will not be long before we will be paid off again, as the government owes us two months pay the first of next month, and I hope that it will be the next pay day. if it should, it will give you a chance to get you and the children some nice summer clothes, as I will be able to send you some thirty five or forty dollars, as I will get my extras then. I got some this time but not all. I sent within two dollars of what my pay came to without the extras. I have kept some seven dollars for my own use, as I have seen how badly a man needs a little money in case he gets sick, which I hope I will not.

the boys are all like me in the best of spirits, all haveing had the blues, but the sight of green backs makes them all jubilent. I am a going to try to send this up as far as Bellford and by our sutler Mr. Tomlison and let him express it from there to you in Wesleys care. I think it the safest way, and it will cost the least.

well, I must tell you I have slept two nights, all night, a something that is very uncommon for me to do. we sent all of our sick up the river on day before yesterday, and we havent had any bad cases sent in since but are expecting some every hour.[61]

well, I expect you have all had a great time reading those notes and letters that I sent home by Capt. Eaton. well, I will have a lot more to send one of these days if the rebels dont get hold of my carcass.

The talk here now is that we all go across the country some forty miles to a place called carthage on the mississippi below Vicksburg and cross the river there and move upon Vicksburg from below,[62] and then another rumor is—and I think it the most probable of the two— is that our brigade or division will be left here as a provost guard to guard this point and Richmond, a little town twelve miles back of here and on the route that all of our supplies have to go through for the army when it gets below us.[63] I hope that we will be left here for I dont like to march one bit, I dont. it makes me so tired and sore, but if I have it to do I am in just as good a condition to do it as I have been since I have been in the service, and then I have no gun and acoutrements to carey, which make about forty pounds.

if I can get the chance I will send my own coat home and one of my blankets, if you think you can keep them, as I heard a letter read that stated they were searching all the houses and taking all the guns, overcoats, blankets, and clothing that the soldiers send home. if it is the case I want you to send me word, and I will not send mine home, as I dont think the government has any right to take what I have paid for.

The weather is butifull, and the men are all in good spirits. give my love to all and write imeaditly, as I want to know how this precious little package gets home, as I am shure it will as I will express it by Adams express if I cant send it the other way that I spoke of. tell cap[tain] eaton [to] write. My love and respects to all. good by. From Yours Afectionately. Wm. Winters

# FOUR

# "We Whiped the Rebels Badly"

In mid-April 1863 Grant's army began a campaign that would last two and a half months and end in the capture of Vicksburg and the thirty-thousand-man Rebel army of John C. Pemberton. The first month of the campaign was one of rapid and almost continuous movement and frequent, uniformly successful combat. It was hard but exhilarating, and Winters was elated at the army's success.

The last six weeks of the Vicksburg Campaign were spent in siege operations, filled with danger, boredom, and discomfort. Winters and his fellow soldiers had plenty of time to reflect on how far they were from home and how long it would be until they would see their families again. Of several patients in the field hospital where he still worked, Winters wrote, "They would get well in a short time if they wasnt quite so home sick."

Winters himself struggled with the boredom and the homesickness, and at times he got desperately tired of the war, the army, the country, and all that stood between him and his peaceful Indiana home. "I dont know when we will get out of this southern country even after we take Vicksburgh," he wrote during the siege, "but I hope it wont be long for I am tired of it." He was tired of the fighting too. "I am tired of seeing men mangled to death as I have to every day," he repined.

Hearing from the folks back home was one of the few things that made the situation tolerable. A letter from home was like a swallow of cool water in a burning emotional desert, and Winters and his fellow soldiers lived from mail-call to mail-call. "Write soon, write soon, write soon & often[!]" he wrote across the margin of one of his letters to Hattie.

Yet even boredom and loneliness did not completely dim his characteristic interest in the world around him. Indeed, the intense interest he took in nature was probably second only to letters from home as a means of helping him to deal with the uglier facets of his situation. Noticing a strain of pumpkins he liked growing locally, he procured some seed and sent his wife "some secesh [secessionist] pumkin seeds." And although he might often write, "I am tired of this country," he could also comment on the abundance of blackberries nearby and opine, "This must be a butifull country to live in in the time of peace and quiet." It would see precious little of either, however, during the campaign in which Winters was about to take part.

Milliken's Store, April 13th, 1863

Dear Wife, I sit me down this morning to write you a few lines, the last that I shall be able to write you from this point, as we have to move tomorrow. our destination is carthage, below vicksburgh. we have a forty mile march before us, but that is not all we have, for so far as I am informed we have the biggest fight of this rebellion, and that before we see the Mississippi again. our forces have had some pretty hard skirmishing already. the rebels are said to be in heavy force and determined to contest the right of way with us before we get on the other side of the river, and they will be shure to after we have crossed. you will hear some news from this army before long, and it will either be that it is badly cut to pieces or that Vicksburgh is ours, as there is a tremendous army down here now. twenty boat loads of troops came down on yesterday to take a hand in the dreadfull strife and help the old flag.

our forces have brought in 471 bales of cotton since last saturday morning, besides some 200 cattle. they also captured a rebel Lieut Colonel and a captain with some privates on last friday in the skirmish that come of this. the rebel prisoners were all wounded that were brought in at this point.

Hat, I dread the march before us, as it rained all night last night hard and driseled all day yesterday, and it has kept it up all night to night and is raining still.

it is now just 17 minutes after three oclock, and Mike Lewis wants me to wet his arm again and give him a drink of water.[1] he shot his left arm badly on last saturday night while out on picket. he was standing with his gun carelessly across the back of his neck with his right hand on the brich [breech] and his left on the bayonet, when the[y] thought they heard something making a fuss behind them and turning quick to see what it was he hit the hammer of his gun against a tree and discharged it, the ball passing through his arm just above the wrist, shatering the upper bone all to peices. Doctor Chitendon, our brigade surgeon, and Dr. Dodds and bryon[2] performed the operation on Sunday morning, taking out the upper bone from the wrist joint back about four inches and resetting the lower bone so as to save his hand, I think, unless he gets unflamation in it. if he does, he will loose it.

we have 21 sick in the hospital now. the[y] will all be put aboard of a boat and sent to some general hospital. Charley Bannes is here sick with the diareah, also Elijah Dudly, but they are not bad. we have had some verey fine wether for about two weeks untill sunday night, and now it is for the other way.

I received a letter from Mrs. Wooden asking me about her brother Permenas Lick.[3] I must answer it to night yet and send you the one I got from her. I haven't received anything from you since Capt Eaton left. I wish that I could get what letters there is on the way from home to me, but that I canot do, and when we will get them after we leave here is more than I can tell, if we ever get them at all, but fate only knows what is in store for a soldier. we are here now, but where we will be when you get this is something else, but I hope that we will get through without the loss of many men.

Well, I must hurey and finish as it is getting late, and I can write but a few minutes at a time. I sent you $50 dollars in greenbacks, and this morning I will send you my overcoat, one blanket, and my dress coat. I will keep my boots as it is so dreadfull wet and mudy I could not march with my shoes on without having my feet wet all the time, and I dont want to risk my health. I am well now and hope that this may find you all enjoying the same most precious boon. Give my love to all and write soon, direct as usual, and the letters will follow us. I sent three roses to vin in a letter; tell her to give one to you and one to mary Jane. I will put some secesh [secessionist] pumkin seeds in this and I want you to give them out as you think best. Only be shure and give wes some. From your afectionate husband.

Wm. Winters

P. S. tell wes that Dr. dodd has resigned and will go home in a day or two.[4] Bill

in Camp at Barrows Plantation, Hines [Hinds] County,[5] Mississippi, May 14, [1863]

Dear wife, it has been some time since I wrote, but it has [been] so unavoidably. we left Millikens bend the day after [I] wrote my last, and we have marched constantley ever since. We have had a fight since then which lasted all day, but we whiped the rebels badly.[6] you have probably read the whole account before this as [this line illegible]. we are now some 21 miles from Vicksburgh and behind it in the same state. Our forces had a fight with the rebs on day before yesterday and sent them flying in the direction of the citty.[7] we are in the reserve and guarding the wagon train.

I got a letter from Dr. Boington[8] last night. it was a good long one and had a good deal of news in it and was quite a treat. You can bet I got a letter from you since I left the Bend [Milliken's Bend] and one from [illegible] who [illegible] was complaining a little. he said he thought it was worse. I hope she is beter now.

I am in very good health at present but am verey sore from marching. I was on the battlefield from 8 o'clock until dark. It was the handsomest fight that I ever expect to witness. I could see the maovering [maneuvering] on both sides and it was a terible days work. We had marched from 12 o'clock at night and got to the battle field at 7 in the morning, and I got out onto the field at 8 to look after our wounded men. The 67[th] lost no men at all, being held in reserve.[9]

the boys are all in good health, but Eli Zigler, he is complaining with diareah.[10] our mail starts back in a few minutes, and I must close. Elijah Dudley is dead.[11] he died in hospital at the river. C. Bannes is there, but I haven't heard how he is.[12] tell Doc that I will answer his as quick as I can and Viras also. Give my love to all. Tell Wes that I got his letter and will write as soon as I can.

"We Whiped the Rebels Badly"

{53}

From yours affectionately

Wm. Winters

to H. J. Winters

we are in Hines [Hinds] Co., Mississippi

in Camp, back of Vicksburgh

May 25, 1863

Dear wife, I can only write you with a pencil, as pens and ink are played out.

well, we are here—what is left of us. We have had four fights since we have been in Mississippi, and the one that is going on now has been progresing for the last week. we have lost one killed out of Co. I, little Henry Bruner,[13] and we have 3 wounded—Charley Riley,[14] wounded in the arm, arm broken by one of our own shell bouncing and striking him on the left arm below the elbow, crushing the bone; Ad Crisler[15] two first fingers of the right hand taken of[f] at the midle joint; old Billy Blair[16] under the ball of the foot. None of them are serious. Our Regiment has lost about 45 killed and wounded.

I am not very well and have but a few minutes to write in. I will write again in a day or two. this is written while canon and musketry are both at work doing their work of death.

Give my love to all

Wm Winters

P.S. we will be in the city of Vicksburgh before you get this beyond a doubt. This is an awfull country, rough, hilley, broken, and ragged.

We have plenty of wild plums, mulbureys, and strawbereys all ripe and nice. Write, for I am in a hurey to hear from home.

Wm. Winters

I send this in a rebel envelope, and I will send you two rebel postage stamps and a couple of garfish scales. Give wes a couple and Joe some. Bill

Camp in Field, Siege of

Vicksburgh, May 29, [1863]

Dear wife,

I will write again to day as I have got the chance to do so, and I may not get as good a one for some time again, and then if you are as ancious to hear from me as I am to hear from you, you wont care how often I write. This is a fine day. it has rained 2 little showers this morning. It is noon now, and you, I guess, are about sitting down to eat your dinner, and [I] wish that I was there to help you eat it, as I could relish it better than I can sow belley and hard tack, as the boys call it, no matter how poor your dinner is. I know that you have got some good bread and butter, as something I havent seen since I left the river over a month ago.

We have had some hard times since we have been in the state of Mississippi, but I think that we will be in Vicksburgh before a great while, and then we can hear from home a little more direct and get a little more of a variety to eat. We are all verey anxious to see the rebels yeald the works here so that we can get a little rest and some of the comforts of life from the river.

I am going to try and get a detail to go up the river when our wounded are sent away if I can, and if I succeed I dont think they will get me down here again verey soon, as I am tired of this country. The water is not good, and then it dont agree with me to lay out upon the ground and in the open air. I can get along verey well, but it dont like to lay, and I am not verey well. I have been bothered with the diareah for some time.

the boys are all getting allong verey well. I heard from Charley Bannes, and Tom Eaton, Field McCalib—they are all getting well.[17] I believe our wounded are all doing verey well. I got a letter from wes and one from old lady Mullen, and I was verey glad to hear from both of them and to hear that you are all well. You have read all about the diferant fights that we have been into since we came into this state so I will not attempt to write any thing about them. I will put this in a rebel envelope made of wall paper, and I want you to save it and the one I sent you last also, as it was secesh [secessionist]. I have just finished an answer to Revr. Mr. Mullens letter, also to Wesley. I sent his by Dr. Bryan. Tell wes he has resigned and is no longer in the U.S. service. we are in a bad fix now in the 67[th] for surgeons, having none at all. Dodds and Bryon both resigned and Garrish is at home so we are left alone in our glorey. Dr. Burton and Dr. Dean are acting in the capcity of surgeons but they are but poor excuses. Dean is merely hired for a short time.[18]

it is raining again. if you have not lost all the letters that I have sent home, I wish you would save them for me.

I must close. I will try to write more in my next. Give my love and respects to all and write by return mail. I have a letter to answer for vine and one for Dr. Boington. This is 3 to day. write all the news. From your anxious husband

Wm. Winters to my wife

H. J. Winters

Kiss the children for me and tell Molly to tell Mary Jane she must be [illegible]. I send you two geranium leaves from back of Vicksburgh. Bill


In Camp, Seige of
Vicksburg, June 9, 1863
Dear wife,

We are still tunneling away at the rebel works around the city and in same position as we were when I last wrote to you, with a fair prospect of remaining so for several days to come, but we will go into the city of Vicksburgh after awhile, that is shure, for we can live outside of their works longer than they can inside of them, that is certain, for we can get everything we want, and they can get nothing atall. We hear all kinds of rumors of how they are suffering for the want of water and provisions, but we cant tell which tale is the true one, and so we lett them pass for what they will fitch.

The only thing we have here that we can rely on for certain is the roar of cannon and the rattle of musketry, but we have been taking it perfectly cool and easely since the day of the charge.[19] if you where [were] here some time you would not think that we were face to face with an enemy, the men whistling and singing, sutlers selling their wares, and everything looks as if we were in camp for a big rest instead of beseigeing a rebell city.

The worst thing here is the watter does not agree with the men. A good many of them are complaining with the diareah. Jacob Shut, Emanuel Sawers, and Levi Snyder are here in our hospt.[20] they are trying to get Shut and Sawers furloughs for twenty days, but I dont know how they will succeed, but I hope the[y] will get them as they ought to have them.

The weather for the last three days has been most intolrably hot. It looks a litle like rain to day. I hope that it will as we need it. Tom Eaton, Charly Bannes, and the rest of the boys that we left back at the river sick have all got well and are here with the regiment. I believe that the boys are all well but the three that we have here in the Hospt.

the boys are all verey mutch put out with Cap[tain] Eaton. They say that he promised to write to the most of them but he's never wrote a word to the company attall. We all hope that he is doing well. Letters from home are a scarce thing here now. We get the news from the cincinnati, st. Louis, Memphis, and Chicago papers every few days, but this is all. We got a mail the other day that had three letters in it for the 67[th] Reg. And that was all. Three letters in three weeks for three hundred and fifty men is a heavey mail I think.

I am not verey well and dont expect to be untill I get away from this watter. I have written this makes seven letters since I have received on[e] from any person, but I reckon the next mail will be full of them. I hoope that we will be in Vicksburgh before I have to write again. give my love to all. Tell them I eat as many ripe blackberreys as I wanted on day before yesterday. Write soon. From your Afect Husband

Wm. Winters

Camp in Field, Seige of
Vicksburgh, June 12, [18]63

Dear wife, I received yours of May the 28th about three hours ago and take the sheet of paper you sent me and send you an answer forthwith. You will have received three letters from me before you do this if you get all I sent you, and I hope you will as I sent some curiousities home in them. I have written twice to wes and to Vine since I received an answer from either of them, but I am looking [for letters] from them all the time now, as we get a mail now every few days. So you need not feel at a loss to write, as you will be shure to get answer for everyone that you write. I am glad to hear that you are all well and have got your room papered and your garden growing. I would have given a good deal to have been at home on my birthday. I wrote you a letter the day before.

We are still in the rear of Vicksburgh and pounding away at the rebel fortyfications. All the letters that I have sent home for the la[s]t four weeks I want you all to keep as they were all written amid the roar of canon and the rattle of musketry. You can easily imagine me sitting in a hollow and in plain view of the rebel works writting to you all by the music of canon and muskets. If I was at home, I could tell you all, all about it but I cant write it on paper as it would be contrbrand, so you must guess at our situation.[21]

the boys are all doing tolerably well excepting Jake Shutt, Levi Snyder, & Emanuel Sawers. We have them here in a temporary hospital and are doing the best we can for them and the rest of our sick of the Regiment. Jake has gone up to the Division Hospital with Capt. Friedly[22] to be examined by the bord of MD. Directors for a furlough. If he gets one I will send this up by him; if not I will have to mail it.

we are all in good spirits and dont care for the rebels [illegible] from where they come, as we are here to take Vicksburgh, as we can live out here as long as they can in Vicksburgh, for we can get evereything we want, and they can get nothing at all.

I saw Elij McGlocklin and Hen on yesterday. They are both well and send you and wesleys folks their best respects. You wrote that Mary Jane had written to me before you wrote yours. I have not got it yet but hope I will before long as I want to get all the letters that are sent to me, as it is all the real comfort that I see is while I am reading letters from home. You wrote that you did not want me to be uneasey about you or take aney notice of what was written about soldiers wives. Now I havent heard of a word being written about any one and should take no notice of it if I did unless they wrote to me about you. You wrote about some miniatures [photographs] that you sent to me. I dont know what ones you mean unless it is the one that I have got and have always had of yours and the children. If you have sent me any other ones I have not heard a word about them and want you to write all about them as soon as you get this and be shure to write all the particulars about them: who they were and when you sent them.

Give my love and best respects to all and answer by return mail.

From Your Afectionate

Husband Wm. Winters

Kiss the children for me.

Camp in the field, seige of
Vicksburgh, June 17th, [18]63

Dear wife,

Well, we have the good news today that we are to be paid off for two months. I supose that wont make you mad atall to get a litle money to keep you from want while I am gone. I have just finished a letter to philip gambold and thought I would write another to you although I havent received one since my last was written. if you all get the letters that I have written during the seige of this place, I know it wont be very long between times.

Lieut. Akin[23] heard yesterday that his mother was dead. Henry Shults[24] got a letter to that effect. We are all getting along verey well considering the time of year. Jake Shut is getting better. Emanuel Sawers and Levi Snider are about the same, both rather home sick. It has been most awfull hot here for several days, but the boys stand it first rate. The nights are cool, and a fellow feels like keeping his blanket over him. I want you to tell me in your next wether Capt. Eaton called and left the letters and note book that I sent home by him. We all think he has treated the company rather shabily by not writing.

There is more heavey fireing going on to day than there has been since last Sunday.[25] the rebs will have to come to it before long, as we are getting our rifle pits so close to their forts they cant look out atall without putting their heads in the way of our sharp shooters and pickets.

It is nearly noon, and I will stop untill after diner.

Well, Hat, the news is since diner that we dont get paid off untill day after tomorow, so I will finish this and then send another by express when I send my money home, as I will send the most of it to you, as we will have two months pay due as [us] again the first of next month, and we are all in the hope of spending our forth of July in the city of Vicksburgh, and I think they will pay us off again as soon as the city is taken, and I think that will be before long, as we have our rifle pits up so close to the rebel forts and rifle pits that they cant look out at all without being shot as soon as they show their heads.

Well, I have had a tolerable easey time for a while. I am sufering with these boiles on my arm but that is nothing, as they will get well after a while of their o[w]n acord. The men here are all getting tired of laying around in these hollows and want to take Vicksburgh. I have got so used to the sound of canon and musketry that it sounds strange when ever there is a cesation of fireing for awhile which is very seldom. I saw severall buckets full of nice ripe blackberies to day that I wish I had at home for you. They are plenty down here now. This must be a butifull country to live in in the time of peace and quiet, as everything grows profusely here in a wild state.

I havent got Mary Janes letter yet nor those miniatures that you wrote to me about. I want you to write whose they were when you write again. I will send you thirty dollars and as mutch more as I can.

The canonading this after[noon] is terible. Our artilery are fireing solid shot at the rebel forts this afternoon to batter down their forts and brest works. I would give a good deal to be at home on the foruth to eat dinner with you all. Give my love and best respects to all and kiss Edy [Edith] and May for me.

From your afect Husband Wm. Winters

write soon, write soon, write soon & often[!]

June 21, [1863]

Camp, Seige of Vicksburgh

Mrs. Hariet J. Winters

Yesterday we received our money and, to day being Sunday and a cool pleasant day and having a chance to send you some, I will try to answer yours of the 8th, which I received several days ago, but I cant send you as mutch as I sent you word I would as we got no extra pay since the first of March, and that cheats me out of about $15, but I will send you 25 with this. I only drew 26, but I hope that you will have enough to do you untill we are paid again.

we had a lively time of it on yesteday morning. For six hours our artilery opened on the rebel works at six oclock and poured it into them untill thenn, and such a roar of canon as was never heard in this neck of woods before,[26] but the rebs took it all without grumbling, or if they did, we did not hear them, as they seldom answered us, only with musketry, but the thing will come to a crisis before long as we are digging under the front of several of their forts to cave them off, and then they must skedadle, but where to I dont know. We have got some guns in position that throw 8 inch, 9 inch, & 11 inch shell. I saw twelve prisoners that sliped out on yesterday morning to get rid of the preasence of our shell.

It is verey quiet here this morning, and the air is cooll and refereshing and looks and feels like rain. My boils are getting better. I weighed myself last night at the quaretmasters and I wieghed 146 pounds, wich is more than I usualy weighed at home. I hope that this seige will soon be over with, for I am tired of waiting. The boys are all well, I believe, but Shut, Sawers and Snider, and they would get well in a short time if they wasnt quite so home sick. The news here is as scarce as hens teeth and so I cant write any, but I want you to when you write. I dont know when we will get out of this southern country even after we take Vicksburgh, but I hope it wont be long for I am tired of it, but I expect we will have to go to richmond and help Hooker[27] take that place, as it looks as if he cant do it himself. But I hope it will soon be over with, for I am tired of seeing men mangled to death as I have to every day, for where they are constantly fighting it is imposible for them all to escape.

I will send this to Indianapolis by Major Wilson.[28] he is going up and has volenteered to take our money and express it for us from there. it will save you something and come quicker than if I send by express all the way. I will send this in wesleys name so you will not have to go to the office to sign the receipt. I want you to write as soon as you get this so that I will know wether you received it or not. Give my love and respects to all and tell them to write, write, write.

From Your
Afect
Husb. Wm. Winters

FIVE

# *"Vicksburgh Is Ours!"*

The long, wearisome siege of Vicksburg came to an abrupt end when, on July 4, 1863, Pemberton surrendered the town and its Confederate garrison. It was one of the great Union victories of the war and a heavy blow to Southern morale. Within days, the entire length of the Mississippi was under Union control. For the North, for Grant, and for individual Federal soldiers like William Winters, the question was, what next? For the moment, the answer was, wait. New operations had to be conceived, planned, and prepared, and that would take time.

After basking a bit in the glory of victory, Winters and his fellow soldiers settled down to a period of uncertainty. "I dont know how long we will remain here or where we will go to from here," he told his wife, "but I hope it will be up the river, as I want to get where it is a litle more pleasant and healthy." By late August it appeared the army had other ideas. "We have been expecting to go down the river every day for the last three weeks, but we are here yet and cant find out for certain when we will leave or where we will go." And so the days and weeks passed, as Winters and his comrades enjoyed a quiet period inside the city that had so long been their goal.

Division Hospital, rear of Vicksburgh, July 6th, 1863
Dear Wife,
Vicksburgh is ours!

Pemberton surendered on the 4th, and such a day was never known in this country, I know, for we had got tired of laying here in these hollows and pounding without doing verey mutch aparent good, but the rebs had to come to it at last, but they held out as long as they had any thing to eat and actuly eat mule beef before they surendered.

I was down to the city on yesterday afternoon and took a stroll through the town looking at the work of destruction which is visable on every hand. The effects of our mortor shell is frightfull to look at, for where ever they struck they lef a frightful mark. I saw houses that shells from our mortor had struck and went straight down through from the roof to the cellar and the hole was large enough to drop a bushell basket through and some would take out nearly one whole side [illegible]. When they struck the ground before bursting, they left a queer looking hole. Some of them left a place resembling a potatoe hill where the potatoes had cracked the hill all open, only in size they looked as if a cow was buried on the top of the ground. Others again would throw the dirt about and leave a hole that would hid a hogshead, and the efect of the shot and shell in some places is terible to look at. I saw one house that had 27 round shot holes in it and I dont know how many from musket balls and fragments of shell, but it was an awfull sight.

And then the greatest curiosity was the caves in the hill side that the citisens have dug to protect themselves from the deadly misels that our guns were constatly hurling into their midst. They cut them with the roof arched and the side of them trimmed down very smooth, and there [was] this rush carpet laid down to walk upon and nicly tacked around over the walls and ceiling so as to keep their clothes clean; and from the looks, every family in the city must of had one or more as the hills are perfectly full of them. I counted 20 in one roe in one place and sixteen in another, and I had not time to take particular notice. I only saw those that I walked pased.

This city looks dirty and disgraceful, a great many of the residents having left for safer quarters some 2 months ago, and the dust is so deep and dry that it has setled all over everything and gives the place a forlorn and forsaken apearance. And then to see those poor sick rebels lying about dirty and raged! Everything around them looks filthy and greasey and the atmosphere is full of a nasty, sickening, humid smell ariseing from the decaying animal matter and ofals of one kind and another that is laying around in every direction. The quarters where their men stay are perfectly filthy, and their hospitals are but verey litle better. those in the field are no better. I should like to have you see the diferenace between where I have my men quartered at and one of those rebel hospitals, as they cho[o]se to call them. I have my men all upon cots and with bed sacks filled with cotton, a clean white sheet spread over that, and then I made them all put on clen white shirts and red flanel drawers, and they look realey comfortable. And then I keep the tents and quarters swept up clean, and I think if some of those rebel surgeons would come out and look at our division Hospital they would think that our sanitary societies at home were doeing a noble work and they would go back and make their men keep themselves more clean and tidy. We have not nearly the amount of sickness that they have, notwithstanding they are in their own climate and we are not. I saw a great maney that were nearly eat up with the scurvey, something we have not been troubled with as yet, having had only a few cases and those were not bad.[1]

I took a strole down along the levey, and it was perfectly crowded with rebs looking at our gun boats and steam boats. The wharf was crowded for a mile with boats, something that plenty of the rebels had never saw, having lived away back in the interior. And it was amusing to hear the remarks that some of them would make as the sailors from the gun boats would come of[f] from their boats to see what damage their firing had done to the rebel town and fortifacations. Whenever the rebels would see a black sailor with his white pants and blue shirt they would swear at an awful rate.

But the most of them [the captured Confederates] dont want to be paroled at all. They say they want to go north untill this war is over as they are tired of it, or if they cant do that they want to take the oath of alegiance and then go north untill the war is over, as they are satisfied of how the thing is going. Some of them, however, swear that they will fight us as long as they live or have a foot of ground to fight upon, but they are only the fewest [illegible].

We are going to send Joe gambold[2] up the river to Memphis or some other place, as there is no chance for him to get well down here.

the Regiment left yes[terday] in morning for to try old Joe Johnson a fight if he will stop for them to do it.[3] we heard to day noon that [they] had him surounded some where between here and Jackson, but I dont know how true it is.

Well, I guess I have written enough for this time. this is rebel paper that come from Vicksburgh. Give my love to all and write oftener. I haven't received but one letter in three weeks, and there was from wes the [illegible].

Wm. Winter

tell the folks that I am well.

P.S. I wish you had some peaches like I paid a dime for a half a dozen of yesterday—if I had only had some cream.

Bill

Joe gamboled leaves for the river this afternoon.

Bill

What do you think of rebel letter paper? And then what is the matter with Mat Beavers? Is she mareed yet to Jotham Sleare?

Hospital, July 18th, 1863

Dear Wife,

I have got a first rate chance to send a few lines home to you with those likenys [likenesses; photos], and I thought that perhaps I had beter do so as they were wearing out in my pocket and liable to be lost at any time. I send them by Pete Swingle to Columbus, and he will mail it from there.

we have got the news down here that John Morgan is making a raid into Indiana with 8 or 10 thousand men and had got as far as salem and burned the Depot.[4] if such is the case now is the time for the men that are at home that always said the[y] would enlist when the time come—and now is the time—to catch him before he has time to get out of the state. If they ever alow him to get out, I think the state aught to secede at once. if they cant catch him, why, they had better send for us to come and do it for them, for we can.

*"Vicksburgh Is Ours!"*
{66}

But I must hurey as pete is waiting. I could get a furlough but it would cost me $40 to come home and back, and I think it would be a waste of money. And then I think we will all be nearer home this fall any way, and then I will try the experiement. Give my love to all and write soon. Tell all the folks that I am well if they want to know.

From Yours untill Death,

Wm Winters

Vicksburgh, Miss., July 26, [18]63

Dear Wife,

I received your two last letters at the same time, the one that you sent by mr. Allen and the one that wesly wrote for you. It went out to Jackson to the Reg. And Lieutenant Akins gave it to me as soon as they got back from jackson. Frank[5] said you were all well and in good spirits considering the scare that John Morgan gave the folks in Hoosierdom. Now we all think that they all done something brave by letting that rebel pirate go clean through the state without ever compelling him to stop and fight. Our regiment is small, but if they was up there Morgan would have to fight.

Well, hat, we are encamped just below the city and have our hospital tents pitched on the bank of the river with a full view of the lower side of the city, and it looks good to be where we can see something that looks like civilised life again. you can guess how natural it looks to see boats going and comeing and hear the bustle of loading and unloading to me.[6] we have quite a number of sick in the Hospital. Mason Lawless,[7] Levi Snyder, and Billy Madex[8] are sick but none of them are bad of[f] excepting Mase Lawley. He is quite sick. Emanuel sawers is no better than he has been for a good while, but he is not sick. It is only a stifness of his joints in the hips and small of his back.[9]

well, we have just got some late papers with the news that old John Morgan got thrashed and all his men taken prisoners some where in the vacinity of pomroy, ohio.[10] good for the buckeyes, we say, but shame on the hoshiers.

It is a hot day down here, but we have a fine breese from the river making it quite pleasant. I dont know how long we will remain here or where we will go to from here, but I hope it will be up the river, as I want to get where it is a litle more pleasant and healthy.

I saw Hen and Elij McGlocklin this morning. They are both well. Hen was taken prisoner out on the march to Jackson by some of Joe Johnsons cavalry. They marched him around about 150 miles, he says, and then paroled him and sent him into our lines. He says they gave him nothing to eat but green corn.

You wrote that Edith was not very well. I hope that she is better before this, as I dont want to lose another and me away down here. hopeing this will find you all well, I remain your

Afect Husband

Wm Winters

Vicksburgh, Miss., July 31, [18]63

Dear wife, I have a good oportunity of sending a few lines home, and I will take advantage [of] it to send you some money, as we are being paid of[f] this morning and Lieut. Akin is a going up home, I believe, so I will send it by him or Field McCalip,[11] as he is coming home on a furlough. I could not make up my mind to pay 20 dollars to come home for 21 or 30 days, and so I staid here. I dont know how long we will remain here. there is some talk of our going down the river to Natchese [Natchez, Mississippi] to garison the place, but I dont know how it will be. Some say that we will come up the river, but we cant tell where we will go untill we start. Then it will be settled for shure, and then I will write as soon as we stop.

Mason Lawless is very sick, and I think cant get well. The rest of the boys are in good health as a generall thing.

But I am in a hurrey and must close. I am not well to day by a good deal, but that is nothing. Give my love to all and write soon.

From your Afnt Husd

Wm winters

Vicksburg, Miss., Aug. 14, 1863

Mrs. H. J. Winters, Dear Wife

having an opportunity of send[ing] this direct to you by charley Bannus so I concluded that I would not wait for an answer to the one I sent by Anderson Reed. You have received it before you will this, as he left several days ago on a sick furlough. We will not stay here a great while, perhaps a week or two and may be longer, but we dont expect to stay but a short time. if I had of know[n] that we would have been sent below instead of comeing up the river as we all expected to, I should have tried to have got a furlough. but I thought that we woud come up to Kentucky and it would not cost me so mutch to come home of while. But now it is all played out, for I cant tell when I may get the chance to come home now, as we are going to New Orleans. I supose that is certain, as port Hudson is sickly and not a verey good location for a large army to incamp at.[12]

we have no news here at all. The armies are not doing any thing at present that we can hear of down here. I hope that you have more news than we have, as it is almost awfull dull here. I am well and hope that this will find you so. you wrote in your last that you was not well. I hope that you are better now, as it makes me verey uneasey.

I must hurey this to a close, as the ambulance will soon be here after the boys to go to the boat. If you get this before Liet. Akins starts back, I wish you would send me some stamps. Give my love to all and write as often as you can. From Yours until Death,

Wm. Winters

Vicksburgh, Miss., Aug. 22nd, [18]63

Mrs. H. J. Winters

Dear wife, it has been a good while since I received a letter from home, as I havent received a word from home since before Anderson

Reed started home on furlough. I sent you a letter by him, also one by charley Bannuss, both of which I hope you have received before this, if they have done as they agreed to when they left: to take them to you as soon as the[y] got home if they were able to do so and if they could not deliver them in person they would send them by some trusty person so that you would get them as soon a[s] posible.

When you write, I want you to send me word if Mason Lawless has got home alive and how he is if you can find out, as I had no hope of his life atall, as he was verey low at the time and dreadfuley ematiated in flesh and muscle, and I felt verey mutch interested in his case as I nursed him for a good while. Chrley Banus was verey mutch reduced when he started for home, but he could make the trip verey well, as he was not so badley diseased as mason was when he left. The health of the Reg is verey good at present considering the hot weather and the season of the year.

it is verey near time for Liet Akins to be back again with the men that went home when he did. We have no news of any importance here, only what we get from northern papers, so you se[e] you get all the news about a week before we do. we have been expecting to go down the river every day for the last three weeks, but we are here yet and cant find out for certain when we will leave or where we will go, wether it will be up the river or down. There has been a great maney troops sent down to New Orleans and other points below, and we are all that is left, and there is some talk of us staying here for awhile and perhaps this winter, but I hope not, as I have no desire to spend another winter in the south.

This is the season for yellow fever, but we have not heard of its making its apearance in the army yet, and I think we will not be troubled with the disease this fall.

I have been verey uneasey about you, as you was not well when you wrote you[r] last two letters. But I hope that you have got along without being very sick. I want you to let me know just how you are getting along and what the news is at home. I havent heard from the city [Cincinnati] since I wrote last and dont know how they are getting alon[g] there, but I guess they are all right if the draft dont catch some of them. Aus is safe, as he is in the service already as a pilot. When you write, I want you to let me know wether O'Hanels has been out to see you or not as Robert wrote he was agoing to start to hope [Hope, Indiana] the next day after he wrote his letter. I am not very well. I never had the headache half as bad in my life as I had on yesterday all day. I thought my head would burst. I had a high fever all day and all night but am a great deal better today. I have been taking medecine prety freely and felt as if it was doing its work first rate now. I dont want you to get uneasey about me, for if I get any worse I shal aply for a sick furlough and come home. I send you and one of the children a ring that I mad[e] out of some [illegible] coal that come of[f] from the steamer City of Madison that was blown up at the warf here on the 19[th].[13] Give my love to all and write soon.

From

Wm. Winters

# SIX

# *"Down the River"*

The uncertain and unsettled period at Vicksburg came to an end August 23, when the Sixty-seventh Indiana boarded a steamboat for the voyage down the Mississippi River to the vicinity of New Orleans, Louisiana. Political considerations, not necessarily tied to the goal of defeating the Confederacy in the most expeditious manner, prompted the Union government to send substantial numbers of troops to Louisiana and Texas under the command of Maj. Gen. Nathaniel Preston Banks, a politician seeking military glory as a general.

The immediate practical result for Winters and the men of the Sixty-seventh was more waiting and wondering—but now in a new place, the Louisiana gulf coast. Banks's halting and uncertain use of his forces punctuated their boredom with military disaster in November 1863—a debacle that Winters himself narrowly avoided. His letters home reflect a mixture of homesickness and war-weariness along with wonder and admiration for the strange new land in which he was now stationed. Oranges, lemons, coconuts, "water lettuce," sea shells, and alligators headed the list of the curiosities in this brave new world, but Winters desperately missed his home and family. "This is not home, for all they have oranges and lemons growing in their gardens and front yards," he wrote from Louisiana. "I want to see some Hoosier corn a growing once more."

Seeing children reminded him "of my own two little girls at home." "But they are at home," he lamented, "and I am here and with the disagreable knowledge that I shall not be able to see them for some time and no certainty how long it will bee." And as always for a soldier, there was the boredom: again and again he commented, "it is awfull dull and lonesome," "it is most awfull dull down here in this godforsaken land of rebeldom and miserey." He tried to keep a good attitude when he could and summed up his and his comrades' eagerness to complete their duties and go home when he wrote, "We are all well and in good spirits and in a hurey to put this scrape at an end."

*"Down the River"* {72}

☙

August 31st, [18]63
In Camp at Carol[l]ton, Louisiana
Mrs. H. J. Winters
Dear wife,

I received a letter from you this morning dated at cincinnati Aug. the 12. I was verey glad to hear from you, but the letter done me but verey litle good, as I could not make out what you wrote with any satisfaction. But anything is some relief, for I havent heard from you or any one else for a good while before we left vicksburgh, and I am at a loss to acount for it. it seems to me that the folks must all of concluded to drop writing to me at the same time, as they have not answered my last, none of them. And this makes four or five letters that I have written to you and only got one in return, and that I cant read. It is hard to be this far from home and not be remembered by those we have left behind. There is more complaint in the regiment about mens own wives not writing to them then there aught to be by a good deal, but we are here and they are there so we have to put up with it with the best grace we can no matter how hard it is to bear. But we cant acount for the neglect.

I have no news to write, as we get none—only from the northern papers. I took a trip out to lake ponchetrain [Lake Ponchartrain, near New Orleans] on yesterday after noon on the cars. It only cost me a dime each way, and the trip is well worth the money. It takes about 20 minutes to run out to the lake, and there we can go out and take a salt water swim, as the watter in the lake is slightly salty. It is a nice sheet of water, but the shore is verey swampy, and in high water must be bad to get around atal. Crabs are plenty and easely taken with a small dip net, and fish is as plenty as I ever saw them any where in my life and verey cheap. The rail road from carolton and to the lake runs through the most abomnable swamp all the way that I ever saw in my life. the weeds are so high along the track that I could not see out of the car at all in a good many places. I had to keep my head from the window to keep the weeds and brush from putting my eyes out, as they dont keep them cut away from the rails atall. I saw some pretty litle swordfish darting through the water as I was in bathing, but the[y] were all young ones. I did not get to see aney large fish at all of no kind. The trip was a very good one for my health.

Lieutenant friedley received an oficial notice of Mason Lawlesses death on yesterday. He died at Memphis on the 14 of this month. I did not think he would get home when he started. I have not heard from any of the other boys, and I supose they must of got home or we would of heard from them before this. I sent a letter home by Anderson Reed and one by Charly Bannuss. I sent one to you by mail the day before we left vicksburg with two [illegible] coal rings in it for you and one of the children. If I can get a couple of small files in the city, firs time I go down I will [send] you some of oyster shells as they make a butifull ring and dont break so easily as the coal does. When we get down on the co[a]st, as I expect we will in a short time, I am a going to try to collect some shells for the children, as they have never had aney thing of the kind. I think I can colect some verey butifull specimens along the shore after we leve here, and I dont know how soon we may have to leave this point, as we have orders to be ready to move at aney time.

I was in camp of the 90th New York the other day. there is quite a number of New York Regiments here, and I think that I can find some old acquaintances among some of them. I am a going to try to find some of my relatives if they are here aney where. I havent been down to New Orleans yet, but I am a going in a few days to see the city, and then I will tell you all about it. if I can send home some oranges and lemons and some coconuts by express I shall certainly do it when we are paid off, which I think will be in the course of a week.

We are camped in a very level and pleasant camping ground. The wether is not very hot, and we have a fine sea breese all the time, and the boys are a grat deal better satisfied then they were at vicksburgh. It is not near so hot here as it was there.

I am not verey well. The diareah troubles me more or less all the time, but I dont take any notice of it, as it has never mad[e] me sick yet.

Give my best respects to all and write by return mail and direct your letters to Wm. Winters, Co. I, 67 Ind. Vol., 4th Division, 13 army Corps, Army of the gulf.

from yours untill death,

Wm. Winters.

Put via cairo on the envelope and direct to New Orleans, La.

Camp Champ De Mars, Near
Carol[l]ton, Louisana, Sep[t]. 12, [18]63
Mrs. H. J. Winters

Dear Wife, I have been waiting several days for Henry Shutts[1] to come down from Vicksburgh, but he has not got here yet. Captain Friedley told me he thought that Henrey had some letters for me, as he brought all the letters from Hope. Cap has been here two days now, but henry has not got here yet. He was left behind at Vicksburgh. He wen[t] up in town and did not get back in time for the boat, so we have to wait for aney letters that he may have for the boys, but we are afraid that he will not get here in time for us to answer them before we leave here, as we expect to leave in a day or two. Our troops have met with a reverse at sabine pass, some where on the coast between here and Galveston, Texas, and we have to go there to help them out of a tight place.[2] the third division of our army core started this morning, and we are the fourth, so you see it cant be long before we will go to[o]. we may go tomorow, for all we can tell to day. so for fear of not getting a chance to write after we get orders to move, I thought that I had better write to day.

the last letter that I got from you, you was at the city but said you was going to start home in a few days, so I supose you are there now. I wrote two letters to you and mailed them while you was in the city, and

I hope that you have got them both, as I directed them both home, as you did not write to me that you was going up to the city atall. So I did not know any thing about it untill you was about ready to start home again. I was glad to hear that you got the chance to go up and see all the folks and see what will I hope never be seen in this country again, and that is an armey of men and the work it takes to equip them. I hope that your visit was a pleasant one and that it done you good, as you wrote that you was not well and had not been for some time, which made me quite uneasey all the time, for we are getting farther and farther away from home all the time, and it makes it the harder to go if I think that you are not well, for what would our two little girls do if you were to die and me away off here in the south nearly two thousand miles away from home and not able to get away without a furlough from some generall? But I hope that this will find you well and able to take care of our childrein in my absence.

Field McCalip told me that you had frost in August this year. I am verey sorrey for that, as it must of done a great deal of damage to the late corn and to gardens, but we are all hopeing for the best down here. we all think that if france will mind their own business that we will get home in the spring or the fore part of next summer, but if we have any trouble with france, we dont expect to be discharged before our time is out—if we live that long—and I hope that we all may get home safe.

The weather is very hot down here during the day and verey cool during the night. We have a nice cool sea breese all day here almost everey day, making it quite pleasant in the shade. If it was not for that, it would be verey hot here. it is stiller to day than I have seen it since we have been down here. the boys are all in better health than I have seen them since we have been in the service. we have no bad cases in the hospital at the present time. I have not got mutch to do and [am] in good health so you see that I have a pretty good time of it, or would have if they would pay us off before we leave here, as I am anxious to send you all the money that I can, as you must begin to want some more by this time for I supose you must of spent some of what I sent you while you was at the city.

The boys all hate to leave here, as it is the nicest camp ground that we have ever had, and then they can get anything that they want here at a reasonable price for the money, and then they dont want to go any further away from home; but if we have to be in the south atall I want to be here in the winter time for it must be verey pleasant, but I want to see home again most awfull bad, for this is not home, for all they have oranges and lemons growing in their gardens and front yards. I want to see some Hoosier corn a growing once more.

Field brought me a letter from doc Bointon, but about all he had to tell me was about his fine stud horse and his fine buggy. He said that he sent you the money that I sent home by Lieut. Akin. Now if wes is at home, I want you to ask him what is the reason he dont write, as I wrote last and he has not answered me yet. Tell vine that I wrote two letters to her and directed them both to Frankllin—field [Field Mc-Calip] told me that she was working for Joe Cartes folks—and if she has not got them that she must write aney way. I have made three cocoenot rings, one for you and one for Edith and one for May. I did not know what else to do and so I tried the experiement, and it makes quite a ring. So I mad[e] three for the novelty of the thing. I put them all in this letter for you, and I hope that they will all fit.

Give my love to all and write soon and direct to new orleans untill you hear from me again. I remain your afectionate husband,

Wm. Winters

In late September Winters succeeded in getting a furlough to go home and see his wife and daughters. By late October, however, he was on his way back to the front, and the letters take up again.

Memphis, Tenn., Sunday
Morning, Oct. 25th, [18]63

Dear wife, I am here and all right so far. We have a promise to be sent on down the river from here this afternoon at five oclock, and I hope we willl get of[f], for I dont want to stop on the way aney longer than I can help, for it is not a desireable place to lay at. But we have had good luck so far. We got away from Indianapolis the same day we left home. [We left] Indianapolis at 8 oclock that night, run out to terre haute, and had to lay there about 5 hours for the train to Cairo, got to Cairo about dark the next evening after we left home, staid there that night, and started down the river the next morning, and arived here last night about 10 oclcock, and slept abord, and this morning went up to the provomarshals[3] office and from there down to fort pickering to the transportation for the balance of the trip and got the promise of being sent on this afternoon and hope that we will not be disapointed, for I am anxious to go on now [that] I am started.

But it was harder to leave you and the children than it was the first time I left you. But I hope that it will not be long before I can come home to stay, with the joyfull sound of peace proclaimed ringing in our ears. But we cant tell how long it may be before this acursed rebelion is put down. But I hope that it will be soon.

It is a verey nice and pleasant day to day, but the sabath is no where in the armey. Jake[4] is siting on the other side of the tent writing to his family. He is the most anxious man to report to the hospital here that I ever saw. It is a pity that he cant get a discharge, for he wants it bad. But you must not say a word about it, for of course he denies it.

I am well and hope that this will find you all the same. Give my love and best respects to all the friends, for I feel verey thankfull for the kindnesses that was shown to me at home. write as soon as you get this and direct to New orleans.

From your afectionate
husband, Wm. Winters

Vicksburg, Miss., Nov. 2nd, [18]63
Mrs. H. J. Winters
Dear wife, I wrote to you from Memphis, also to wes, and now I will write to you from here. we arived here yesterday morning and will have to remain here untill we can get transportation further. We may get away today, but it is owing to when there is a government boat

going down when we get off, perhaps to day and may be in a week. I cant find out untill the order is isued, but I hope it wil be to day, as I am anxious to go on, as from what we can learn our reg[iment] has gone to texas, but we dont know for certain.[5] the boys are all here with me and all well and in fine spirits and in a hurey to get to the reg. Jake Shut says that if there is any enquirey made about his health by any of his friends, tell them that he is getting along as well as could be expected under the circumstances. well now, my opinion is that he is one of the sickest men of the service that I ever saw in my life or I am badly fooled in the man, but you must not tel that I wrote so to you, but he would give a pile if he was out of the biz.

Well, perhaps you would like to know what kind of a trip we had from Memphis to this place. we had rain and raw winds in abundance. It was disagreeable enough for aney body for a couple of days, but after that we had fine pleasant wether. This morning it is disagreeably hot. Here the sun comes down the shortest way. I took quite a stroll yesterday afternoon up and down the hills and around on the fortefications, looking at what there was to see and here what there was to hear, and I had a verey pleasant walk of it if it had not of been for one thing: turn where I would the pretty faces of children met my eyes on everey hand and constantly reminded me of my own two little girls at home, but they are at home and I am here and with the disagreable knowledge that I shall not be able to see them for some time and no certainty how long it will bee, for it may not be during the remainder of my time of service, but I hope for the best and let the worst take care of itself.

but we must get out in town and try to find out when we can get off from here, as I am in a hurey. We are stoping at the soldiers home here, the best on[e] I have seen since I have been out. we have verey good bord, and everey thing looks clean, neat, and tidy. It costs us nothing, but then I cant get over being in a hury to get to the reg[iment] to see the boys and get rid of folowing them up.

tell all the folks that I am well and in good spirits. Give my love to all the friends and tell them that they must be shure to write. I must write to Robert to day; I wrote to wes from memphis. Direct your letters to New Orleans and tell all to do so and write as soon as you get this.

From yours as ever,

Wm. Winters

To H. J. Winters

Vicksburgh, Nov. 6th, 1863

Mrs. H. J. Winters

Dear wife, I wrote to you the next day after we arived here, and now I write again to let you know when I leave here. we will get off from here to day or tomorow morning for New Orelans, and then I will write again from there to let you know when I have to go from there to find the regiment, if it is not there when we get there, and from all that we can learn it has left for Texas, but of that we are not certain, as we have not been able to see aney body from there that knew for certain where it was, and I am in hopes that it is not far from there, if they have left atall.

The soldiers home at this place is the nearest a home for a soldier of aney place that I have seen since I left home. it is in a fine large 3 storey brick house that some old rebel had just built for his daughter to live in and had not quite finished it when we took posession of the place. so old abe just conficated it and turned it into a home for the traveling soldiers. It is in charge of a gentleman and his wife by the name of Foster, and they do all in their power to make it a place of comfort to the boys that stop there on their way to and from their homes. It is mainly suported by the western sanitary commission. They have suplied it with a good religeous librarey, and when we left they gave us all a track [a religious tract] or paper to read on our way and wished us a safe return to homes and families. It done me good to see the old ladies of the house and commision giving out tracts, papers, and testaments and constantly counseling the boys to be christians and brave men for their countrys and families sakes and giving one and all an invitation to stop there again if they should ever hapen to pass this way again.

it has been raining here all day yesterday and last night, making it verey nasty to get around the city. We are going down the river on bord the stern wheel steam St Louis. She is a small craft and we shall be considerably cramped on bord of her, but it is all the chance.

Tell all the folks that we are all well and in good spirits and in a hurey to put this scrape at an end. Give my love to all and write soon as you get this, and I will get some of your leters if not all. from yours as ever, Wm. Winters

[on stationery of "Soldier's Home, New Orleans"]

November 12th, 1863

Dear wife, we arived on yesterday morning at daylight, and I am under the painfull necesity of writing home bad news for the friends at home, as our whole brigade is either killed, captured, or wounded with the exception of forty one is all that I can learn of escaping. Cap-[tain] Friedly and Lieut Aikin are both taken prisoners. They are the only ones of our company that I have learned the names of but there are others that are taken of cours, but I dont know who they are yet.

The regiment was being payed off when they were surprised and taken prisoners. Our companey was about half of them payed when they were atacked. From what I can learn, the boys done the best they could for the rebs before they gave up. they fought them three hours, and the rebs lost more men killed and wounded than we did, but they had to[o] maney men, and the boys were compelled to surender to a superior force.[6]

it is bad acccident to the boys that were taken, as the rebels have stoped paroleing prisoners, and they will have to lay in a rebel prison untill they see fit to let them out on parole, and when that will be I cant say, but I hope for their sake it will not be long. There is several of the boys here in the convalesant camp that were left behind unable to go with the reg[iment] when they left here. Cris horniday[7] and Owen Billiard[8] are here and some others, but you dont know them. The rebels paroled all the boys that were wounded, and Capt Sims of Co. D[9] was wounded through the arm, and he was sharp enough to pass himself off as a private and got paroled as such and left here on last night on his way home. he was the only officer that was paroled, and he would not have been if he had not passed of[f] as a private soldier, as the rebs paroled no officers at all.

Now, hat, you can bet that us fellows that are here are in a sweat. We cant find out what we are to do. the reg[iment] is about played out, and the officers here cant tell what to do with us, so we cant find out wether we are to go to the fragment of our regiment or what we are to do, but I recon [reckon] that we will find out in a day or two, and then I will let you know all about it. you need not write to me untill you hear from me again, as it is to[o] uncertain where we will bee, and in the mean time I will find out all that I can about the boys so as to write it home for the benefit of the families. I understood this morning that the regiment lost sixty men killed, but I cant say how true it is, but from what I can learn the rebs lost the most men. I feel verey sorey for the friends at home, as the uncertainty of who is hurt or killed or who is not is as hard as the worst can be when it comes, but some just suffer, but who they are is more than I can tell you now, as I cant find out. I have just heard that there is some of the boys that were wounded here in a hospital. If so, I can find out something about it.

tell all the friends that we are all well. Give them all my respects. I will write again as soon as I can find out aney thing certain about the missing.

From yours as ever,
Wm. Winters
I am well.


Nov. 14th, 1863
Convalesant Camp, New Orleans
Mrs. H. J. Winters
Dear wife, I am here yet in the great metropalis of the sunny south and have been for a week, and I cant say when we will get away, but the sooner the beter, as I am tired of laying around on uncertainty as we have been ever since we left home, but we will get away whenever these shoulder straped gentlemen se[e] fit to send us. So we will have to take it as it comes.

I have not heard from the regiment so as to give you aney of the particulars more than Cap[tain] Friedly is not a prisoner as I first wrote to you he was, but I have since found out better, but Lieut Aikins is a prisoner in the hands of the rebs, but that is all that I can learn about the companey for certain. I was in two of the hospitals that has some of our wounded in the other day, and one of the wounded men of our regiment told me that there was two wounded men of our company came to the city with him, but he did not know where they were put, and I could not find them, so I dont know who they were. But I guess the most of them were captured. I feel verey sorey for Lieut Akin, as he is not stout enough to stand the trip that he will have to take. From what I can learn, they will have to march some three or four hundred miles and then perhaps have to lay in a miserable rebel prison for some time, and I am afraid it will be more than Bill can stand in the condition he was.[10]

the prospect is now that the regiment will stop at Brashear city,[11] or what there is left of it, for a while to see if the rebs woud parole the boys and send them back to the lines at that place or some where close to it. if they donot do so I think the rest that are left will be sent home to Indianapolis to try and recruit some more men and wait for the boys that are prisoners to be paroled and get home. I hope it will be done, for then I could get some news from home inside of a month. I am awfull anxious to hear from you, but I shant be able to do so untill I get to the regiment, as we cant get aney leters this side of there unless they come here instead of our going out there, but I shall have to wait the will of others, so I might as well take it as easey as I can.

We are quartered in a cotton press that covers a whole square. It is a good dry place, and the boys have to keep it clean, so we are tolerably well fixed, only they dont cook the rations more than half as well as they might, and our board is rather poor, but I have had a good deal worse since I have been in the service and will get worse before I get out again.

to day is Sunday, and there is a meeting going on while I am writeing this, but it is conducted by an old fellow that talks so funney that I cant more than half understand him, and I concluded not to go. I was at a prayer meeting last night, and that is as mutch as I can endure of his talk.

It is a most butifull day and makes me feel like I would give almost aney thing to be at home, but that cant be at the presant, but I hope it will not be long. The news, I believe, is verey good from the front and from Charelston, and I think if old Abe will hurey out the last three hundred thousand men that he called out when I was at home, the thing will wind up so that we can get him inside of the coming sumer.

Now I must tell you I have had some grand old laughs at Charley Bannus and Anderson Reed. This is to[o] big a place for them, and they go gapeing about and making expresions that would make a horse laugh if he could. Charley thinks these big boats down here with such long poles sticking on top of them bang all the boats that he ever saw, and then he says, "Bill, how do the dam things go through the water? I dont see aney smoke stacks, and I dont see how the wind can make them go." and then, "Bill, how the devill [do] the[y] work so maney ropes? By golly there is more ropes on that big one younder than I ever saw in all my life before." And then, "Bill, I tell you that I must write to philip and tell him that his hack is no place beside some of these down here. oh, look there at that woman. She showed her——. Well I guess I have not been out from before, for I have seen more here then I ever saw in my life, and everey time I turn around I see something new." And so he goes on all the time. anderson looks like a stray kitten in a strange garret and is always holering to some one to lookee yonder and loud enough to be heard half a square. But enough of that.

I am well and hope this will find you all the same. I wrote to you before not to answer that untill you heard from me again. now I want you to write as soon as you get this, and I will get it when I go to the regiment or it comes to me. give my Best respects to all and tell them to write as often as they please. Send me Jims adress, and I will write to him. From yours as ever, Wm. Winters to H. J. Winters

Sabath afternoon at New Iberia, Louisana[12]
Nov. 22nd, 1863
Mrs. H. J. Winters
Dear wife,
I fineally got to the regiment, what there is left of it, which is verey few to what there was when I left them at carrollton, but there is more

of them than what I first wrote to you. I arived here this morning and found Louis Hine, John Hagecock, Exra Reed, Emanuel Sowers, Wm Coovert, Isaac Stucker, and John Clark, Henrey Shults, and Capt Friedley all well and safe.[13] the regiment lost in killed, wounded, and prisoners over two hundred, and I can hardly see how aney of them escaped atall from what the boys tell me, but the chief object of the rebs seems to have been to capture the pay masters and our suply train with our battery of artilerey, but they did not succeed, as they got no money nor wagons and but one of our cannon. They captured two of the guns in the first place, and we took one of them back again, and they lost more men in killed, wounded, and pris[on]ers than we did. So you can see that they did not make aneything in the outcome but rather lost if aneything.

I saw cap[tain] Friedley this forenoon, and he told me that he expected to be ordered home in a few days to recruit for the regiment, and if he comes home I will write again and send it by him.

I have to tell you of the death of Field McCalip. He died out at the place the boys had the fight. He was taken in the first place with the dysentery, and then typhoid fever set in and something like gravel, and they was just going to send him back, and he died in the amblance after riding all day in the Ambulance. Louis Hine helped burey him, and he tells me that they mad[e] him a coffin of rich pine and laid him to rest in a far off country away from home and friends, but from what the boys all say they buried [him] verey nicely. All mourn his loss, as he was a brave soldier and a kind messmate and had endeared himself to all by the evenness of his temper and universal kindness to all. He died and was buried at what is called carion crow bayou. Give his wife all the comfort you can in her berevement, for to her he was all, and she must feel the loss much more heavily than we can, and we all truley mourn his loss. He died the firs[t] of this month, and the boys had the fight with the rebs on the third of the month.

He is the only man that the companey have lost since I left them, but I am verey fearfull that Lieut Aikin will never see home again, as he was not well when the fight commenced, and when they had to fall back he undertook to get away, and he ran untill he gave out, when our acting adjutant rode up and gave him his horse to ride, but he was so near give out and sick that he called the adjutant and told him to take his horse, that he could go no further and got off from the horse, and the rebels took him prisoner, and I think it verey doubtful if he ever gets home again, as the rebs were compelled to hurey their prisoners away so fast that he could have had no time to rest before they were compelled to start on a march to fort Tyler in texas, over three hundred miles from where they were taken at, but I hope that he will be able to stand up to it. the wounded that were exchanged all say that the rebs treated them all verey kindley.

Col. Emerson[14] is here and doing all he can to get the regiment sent home to try and recruit some and give the boys all a chance to get a litle rest. All the necessary papers have been sent to Gen Bankses[15] head quarters and I think that we will find out what our fate is in the course of a week or two, but I am afraid that we will not get the chance to come up the river, but I hope we may. There is quite a number of the regiment that are not fit for duty, and I think that they aught to get the chance of comeing up to a healthier countrey if posible.

Now perhaps you would like to know what I think of this country down here. well, in the first place Bras[h]ear city is 90 miles from New Orleans, and it is 80 miles from Bras[h]ear city to New Iberia, where we are now encamped, making it 170 miles from here to New orleans. The countrey from New orleans to Braseir [Brashear] city is low, wet, and marshey for the most of the way and wears a forbiding look, but there is some splendid plantations allong the R[ail]R[oad], but I could not bee compelled to live there. the country from Braseer [Brashear] to this place is not so bad, but still it is to[o] levell for buty [beauty], but there is some verey large and fine plantations allong the bayou that we have to come up. now I must tell you a litle about the bayou. It is a verey narow stream, and in some places it is entirely covered with what is called watter or wild lettuce. It is a floating plant and looks a good deal like what is called velvet plant. I saw a good maney alligators along the shores of the bayou as we come up. some of them were quite large ones. the boys on the b[o]at shot a couple of them as we were runing along. The bayou is verey narow and in some places a man could almost jump ashore from either guard [guardrail of the steamboat] but as I had no inclination to be taken prisoner, I did not try the expiriment. Where we are encamped is at the head of naviga- tion of the great stream.

If I get aney letters tomorow, I will answer them and give you more news. Give my love and respects to all and write as soon as you get this. From yours as ever,

Wm. Winters

we expect a large mail tomorrow, and as none of the letters that I hope you have written have got he[re] yet, I hope I will get one when it comes. Bill

New Iberia, Louisiana, Dec. 4th, 1863

Mrs. H. J. Winters

Dear Wife,

having an oportunity of sending a letter home by Capt Friedly, I thought that I would write once more before I received a letter from you, as I have had but one, and that was in answer to the one I wrote from Memphis, and I am in just an awfull way about it, as I never was so anxious to hear from home and you in my life. but it cant be helped I supose, and I shall have to put up with the negligence of government officials.

The wether down here is fine and pleasant, and we have but verey litel to do. I am staying with the companey but doing no duty, as we have no hospital for our regiment and I refused to go to the post hospital. So I have a prety good time of it, but it is awfull dull and lonesome—no news from home and for all that we know down here our families may be sufering from diseas or for the want of money and we not able to even sypothise [sympathize] with them. But as I said it cant be helped.

But the news here last night was cheering. The several generals of our armey rode through their respective divisions and brigades and told the men that old Gen. Grant had everlastingly thrashed Braggs armey and said that he would be in atlanta, Georgia, in five days, and you should of heard the boys yell.[16] they fairly mad[e] the welkin ring again, and when I went to sleep, which was about 10 oclock, they would break out with a hurah for old u. s. grant and then such a huraing you never heard. But this morning it is all quiet, and no one would supose that the boys were the least noisey.

Their health is generaley good. none of Co. I are sick, and all are in verey good spirits. I have not got over the cold that I caught while at home sleeping with you, but it does not hurt me atall more than my nose is the best friend that I have got. But it will all work of[f] after awhile.

We are lying here between hope and fear as we are afraid that we will have to go around to Brownsville, Texas, and then we are in hope of getting up the river. So you see that we are like a fish out of watter and dont know how to get back again, but we will have to wait the will of others, and I sincerely hope that it will be their will to send our litle squad up the river where you and all the friends could hear from us once and awhile and we could do the same, as it is most awfull dull down here in this godforsaken land of rebeldom and miserey.

We have not got verey comfortable quarters, but we have fixed us up a chebang[17] out of plank and covered it with our oil blankets and fixed us up a bunk with a bed of spanish moss, and we are making out verey well.

general Franklin has just sent out a flag of truce to the rebel lines to see if we would be alowed to send our boys that are prisoners some letters that are here for them and to see what could be done for the boys in the way of sending them blankets and clothing. If the truce gets back from there today, Cap can tell the friends something about the boys, but if it does not he knows no more than the rest of them that are here, and that is that the boys are prisoners. I hope for the benefit of the friends of the boys that we will hear from them before cap leaves, as I know that they are all verey anxious about them.

This makes 18 letters that I have written to hope [Hope, Indiana] and cincinnati and have onley got the one from you that I wrote to you about. Enclosed in this you will find a rose that I plucked on thanksgiving day and forgot to put it in the letter that I wrote to you that day. now I want you to keep on writeing, as I will get some if not all of them after awhile. Give my love and respects to all and tell them to write as often as they can make it convenient. I wish we had our pay so that I could send it home by cap, but we have not got it and cant tell when we will get it either, but I hope for your sake it will not be long. From yours as ever, Wm. Winters

Algeirs, Louisiana,[18] Dec. 17th, 1863

Mrs. H. J. Winters

Dear wife, I got a part of my pay last evening, and I could not get over to new orleans myself, and I sent my money, or twenty dollars of it, over with him and instructed him to buy a check and send it to you in the care of Dr. Stapp, and you can get the money for it of any of the merchants of hope [Hope, Indiana], as it will be the same to them as cash, and then it gives us this advantage: if it gets lost we can get another, and whoever finds that cant use it, as it will be useless to anybody else but you. Dr. Stapp can tell you how to get your money for it. we concluded not to express our money as it would cost us about one fourth to express it, and then they wont be responsible for it if the boat burnt or the rebs sink it, and by sending it this way we can get another check if this one gets lost.

Well, hat, it is a blustery bad morning, and the wind is chilley, and my fingers are cold, and I am shivering, and the wind blows so that I cant set out by the fire to write. So I have to take the tent for it and did the best I can, and I thought I had better write this morning for fear that I would not get the chance to write again before we leave here, as we are under marching orders and expect to go abord of a steamer this afternoon or tomorow morning for Texas, and I think after we get these they will pay us the other two months pay that they owe us, and then I will send you more.

last night was an awfull one. It blowed a huricane, rained, thundered, and lightened all night at an awfull rate, and our tent leaked, and the boys in the regiment was all about half tight [drunk] and hooping and yelling, and between them and the storm we got but litle sleep, the few of us that had respect enough for ourselves and families to keep sober. This morning the most of them have begun to lay plans how to get whiskey to take a farewell spree on before they leave for Texas, and to night I expect that they will have a tareing time if we stay ashore.

I dont know what part of Texas we are to go to, but this will probably be the last letter that I shall get the chance of writeing to you from this place. but I shall write again as soon as we get to our destination, be that where it may—that is, if the vesel dont get wrecked and I be devoured and eat up alive by a big fish or a sea sarpint.

Well, we have just got orders to embark on bord a steamer, and of cours that settles the question: no more writing from this place. but it will note [not] tak[e] but about three days to make the run, and then I can write again. I dont know what vesell we are to go aboard of, or I would send you the name so that you could see by the papers how we made the trip before I could get a letter back home again. now I want you to use the money I send home to suit yourself, and I will send you some more as soon as I can. Give my love to all and write soon. From yours

as ever, Wm. Winters

to

H. J. Winters

# SEVEN

# "This Delectable Point of Sand"

Part of the Federal effort in the southwest involved temporarily placing a substantial force on the Texas coast, and that brought Winters's division to the Matagorda Peninsula, a fifty-mile-long sand spit never wider than a couple of miles, connected to the mainland at its northern end and otherwise separated from it by Matagorda Bay. The bay is about five miles wide in most places, but toward the southern end of the peninsula, the mainland coastline falls away to form a bay more than a dozen miles across. Access to this more or less sheltered body of water was by way of Cavallo Pass, a narrow strip of water that separates the peninsula from Matagorda Island, further southwest along the coast. At the southern tip of the peninsula, on the edge of Cavallo Pass, was Point Cavallo, and there the Sixty-seventh Indiana was stationed. Somewhat over ten miles away on the mainland shore of Matagorda Bay was the thriving town of Indianola, Texas, in Union hands since October 1862. After the war, a hurricane demolished Indianola, and it was never again the important commercial center it had been.

Far from the scene of any significant action, Winters and his comrades had very little to do. His letters home reflect his usual mixture of homesickness and war-weariness, fascination with the strange new

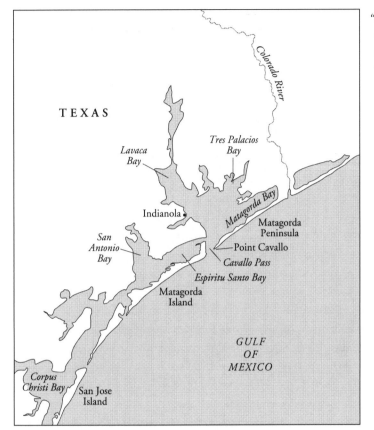

The Texas coast

land in which he found himself and longing to leave it and get back to Indiana and home. Though he sarcastically referred to Point Cavallo as "this delectable point of sand," he was more prone to call it "this miserable piece of sand," and to wonder "how long we shall be forced to disgrace" it. The sand got inside his shoes and clothes and chafed him. "I am so confounded full of sand," he complained, "that I cant hardly keep my skin whole." He and his comrades got to longing for the sight of trees, and part of an unusually hard march up the peninsula was eased by the distant sight of woods on the mainland. "You would have thought that we were a lot of little boys if you had of seen us streach our necks and stand and look at the woods 8 or 9 miles of[f] but to us it was quite a sight." Another sight Winters missed was that of midwestern womenfolk, and this led him to express himself in rather unflattering terms regarding the Texas variety: "What few white women I have seen since I have been in texas look more like digger indians than they do like what they are intended to represent, and as greasey and dirty as a soap boiler."

Winters was very clear as to what was detaining him on this curious but on the whole not very inviting piece of real estate: the Rebels' continued refusal to give up. He often speculated about how long the Southerners could go on fighting "on nothing and for nothing," but he discounted bold Confederate pronouncements of determination to die in the last ditch and in doing so thought something profound: "They will do just as we would if we were in the same fix." Sooner or later they would get tired of the game and give up.

The Texas gulf coast had its charms and fascinations nevertheless, and Winters took an almost boyish delight in them. "I have the bigest crabs claw that you ever saw, I know," he excitedly wrote to Hattie, "and then I have one other curioisity to you, and that is a sea hog or a hog fish, as they are generaly called." These, along with numerous seashells and several rattles from rattlesnakes (he assured her the rattles were harmless), he promised to box up and send home. Still, even the most pleasant times by the balmy Gulf of Mexico tended to remind him of how much he missed home. "We are loling around our tents in the shade watching the tide as it comes rushing toward the shore and listening to the breakers as they break upon the sand and go back to come up in another vain atempt to break over the sandy shore in their made career. It is a butifull day, and I sit here and look at the gulf and think of home, and then I wish—but it is a vain wish, for still I am here on this far of[f] distant shore but still hopeing that this will not be always, and then to me it will not be naught but the dull old gulfs continued roar but the voice of Home and my litle ones."

His "litle ones" were, as always, much on his mind. The reader is constantly impressed with how important they were to him, how little there is about him of the austere and distant father of nineteenth-century stereotype, even if he was sadly and unavoidably distant geographically. While stationed on the Texas coast, Winters even wrote letters to each of his two young daughters, neither of whom was apparently yet able to read or write. He urged them to communicate with him by having their mother write their thoughts into her letters, and his chief fatherly admonition, aside from the natural one to "be good," was to study hard and learn to read.

His much desired homecoming was still in the indefinite future. When that day came, he promised, "We will fix the thing all up again and forget that I ever was away among the rebel states so long. And then I can tell you all about where I have been and what I have seen in the suney south and in the land of dixie."

Point Cavallo, Texas, Jan. 2nd, 1863 [1864]

Mrs. H. J. Winters

Dear wife, I received a letter from you on last evening, written by Wesley, dated Dec. 10th, and I was glad to hear from you and all the rest, as I had received my 3 letters before I got the three that I received last night. One of them was from you, the other from wes, and one from my old friend E. J. Porter, the first word of news that I have received since I lef New Iberia and the first mail that we have received since we arrived here. this makes the third that I have written from this delectable point of sand to you besides what I have written to others, but how lon[g] it will be before I receive answers to them all is more than I can tell or any body else can, for in the first place we have to wait the pleasure of the friends at home and then the pleasure of our miserable mail agents and then the last is the state of the wether on the gulf. so you see that we are not verey certain of hearing from home very often.

Well, hat, we had one of the awfullest marches the other night that I have ever taken in my life. we had been at work the night before all night unloading a battery of guns of[f] from the steam ship St. Mary and had all just gone to bed the night after when we were called out to go on a scout and a foraging expedition. So out we rolled and put on our traps [equipment] and off we started about eleven oclock and marched about 10 miles and halted about 2 hours, and the wind was blowing a huricane, and the sand drifted into our eyes, ears, and mouth like sleet, and the wind was piercing cold, and I had no over cout, and I could not keep warm to save me, and I was tired and sleepy, having been up two nights all night, and then I never in all my life suffered with the cold so or half as mutch, for I thought I would perish in [spite] of all I could do. we started of[f] again just at daylight, and I finealy got warmed up a litle, but I hope that I will never be compelled to suffer so with cold again in my life. but it is all over with now, and we are in the best of spirits and health. We marched just 30 miles in eleven hours and layed by two hours of the time, and I call that big work over this soft sand and through such a storm as we went through and all of that for a drove of sheep.

Well, hat, I have not sent of[f] the box of shells yet, but I have them all boxed up ready to start as soon as our express agent comes back. I have some nice ones. one that I have marked for your new years gift is a verey handsome shell, and then they will be so pretty for the children to play with, and they can pass off maney a lonesome hour playing with their shells if I can only get them home to them.

Well, there is one other thing that I must tell you. I have been promoted since we got here to fourth sergeant of our company. the position advances my pay to 17 dollars a month, which is a litle better then 13 dollars a month, as you need all you can get. I want you to let me know wether you got the check that I sent you from Algiers

[Louisiana]. I expect to be paid of[f] again before long again and then I will get 34 dollars instead of 26 for two months and everey litle helps, you know. I want you [to] tell Bell if she dont answer some of my letters I will make her throat sorer than it is the next time I see her. But I am very sorry for her in her aflictions and hope that she will soon be better. the boys are all well and in fine spirits and hope that this will find you and all the rest the same is the wish of your most humble and tumble down,

from yours as ever, Wm. Winters

In Camp at Point Cavallo,
Texas, Jan. 14th, 1864
Mrs. H. J. Winters

Dear wife, it is a good while since I heard from you, and I am getting most awfull anxious to hear from home to know how you are all gitting and wether you received that check that I sent you from New Orleans and sent you from there for twenty dollars, and I have not heard from it since and dont know wether you ever received it or not. I think that we will be paid off here before long, and then I will send as mutch as I can from here. I will have 34 dollars comeing to me this pay day, and I can send you 30 of that. I hope that they will get that bill through that they have before the House, for it would make my wages 20 dollars a month instead of seventeen as it is now. But seventeen is better than thirteen. but I want all I can get. If it is a hundred I will not gravel about it at pay day.

Well, the wether is once more warm and pleasant again, and I feel all right. But the way it made us squat about a week was not to be gained at, and the way the boys wished that they were at home at [illegible] was funey to listen to, and the worst of it was our rations got most confounded short, and a good maney of the Reg[iment] had no bread for a week, and between that and the cold north wind, we had a butifull time of it and no mistake, but it has all pased over, and we have plenty again. a vesell came in night before last loaded with crocks [of] meat, dried fruit, onions, and potatoes, so you see we will have a feast as soon as it is all unloaded and distributed to the diferant quartermasters, and then we can make up for our litel fast that we was compelled to take. But our companey did not get out of bread at all, but some of the others in our Reg[iment] were out for four days. We run out of coffe and sugar and had but a slim alowance of meat, but we made out by buying some coffee and sugar of the suttlers at a dollar a pound for coffe and 25 cents for brown sugar, and I believe that the coffee had been boiled once, for it was the weakest stuff that I ever saw or drank in my life, and then it was not pure coffe. But you see the suttlers could not get rich fast enough if they did not cheat the boys in every way they can.

But I guess that will not make aney diference after the war is over, and our forces are giving it to them here now. We have been listening to an engagement between our forces at indianola and the rebs for a couple of days, and last night the firing ceased, and to day we heard that our troops had took three hundred prisoners and give the rebs a nice litle drubing for putting their bill in where it did not belong. But I have not heard what the loss was on either side, but I think we will hear to night or in the morning. If we do, I will make a note of it on the margin of this sheet somewhere before I mail it to you.[1]

I picked up some litle small shells on yesterday, and I will put some of them in this letter for the fun of the thing, as I have the box that Charly Bannes and I have ours packed in all nailed up, and I dont want to open it again. I put in one large raged looking shell with your name on it in pencil marks, and that I want you to keep for your New Years gift if they ever get hom. But we have not started them yet, so you need not look for them for a while yet, for I dont think that they will be apt to come untill we start them. And it may be that they will never get through when we do.

Well, we had a big inspection here on yesterday and one to day by our new general.[2] he is a young man, but I think that he is [a] verey fine man and looks to the interest of the men that he has under his co-mand, for he was verey pleasant with us, and when ever he found any of the boy['s] guns in a bad fix he would ask them if they was well and then with a smile tell them that their lives depended upon their arms and it was best to have them in good order and clean, for a dirty gun might be the means of a rebs getting the advantage of them, and then a soldier's name depended upon his aperance a great deal, and the most of all the nation depended upon us and we upon our guns—boys, keep them clean, and if there is aney thing that you aught to have that you havent got, why make complaint to me, and it is my duty to see that you are suplied with all that you need in the field. The boys all fell in love with him, and so did I.

well, it got most awfull foggy here this morning from seven to eight. We could not see each other more than twenty feet, and it looked for a short time as if it was agoing to get so thick that we could cut it out in blocks. But it faded away in about an hour, and now it is warm enough for to do without a coat. But I am afraid to go without mine for fear of chills and fever. I was out on picket the other night, the first time for over a year, and I caught a cold, and my nose is the best friend that I have got here. I had charge of a post and sixteen men, and it was an [illegible] job for me, you better believe. but I got through all right.

And now I must tell you I saw a man the other day of our Reg[iment] that was taken when the Reg[iment] was at carion crow,[3] and he told me that the boys were all at algiers and that three of our company were exchanged and the rest paroled and that all of them were agoing to remain at algeirs, as they had all went into a paroled camp there. so you see we can give up the idea of getting a chance to come home this time. so that is all knocked in the head, and we will have to stay in Texas a while longer. We may perhaps be sent back to new Orleans after awhile if the boys are not exchanged soon, but there is not mutch chance for that, as I know of.

But we are doing verey well here if it was not for wood and watter being so scarce. But I recon we can do like the Irishman did by being hung—get used to it. there is some talk of our brigade being left here for to garison the pont when the armey gets ready to move, but I cant say how it will be. But I hope we will unless the rest of the Regiment is exchanged before that time.

what little news we get here from the north is verey cheering, and I am in hopes that it will continue so, for I am getting most awfull anxious to get home and live like a white man instead of burowing in the sand like a turtle. Now when you write I want you to write as mutch as you posibly can, for I want to hear all that is going on at home and how the draft come off, as I supose it will be over with before you answer this, and I want to know who is the lucky man in our township, for from what I have heard there was not a man that had enlisted up to the 18th of last month.[4]

I heard that cap[tain] friedly and hen shults[5] got to indianapolis on the 18th and went down home on the 19th, so I supose that you have received the letters that I sent by them to you and Bell. I put them both in the same envelope and am expecting an answer to them both in a few days, as it is over a month now since they started and will be a month in a few days now since they got home, and a letter aught to come through in that time [if] you answered as soon as you received them. Bell wrote in her last that Olivers folks wanted you to come down there and stay awhile. If you think that it will be any cheaper, I have no objection atall, and I want you to write if you go before you start and as soon as you get there so that I will know how to direct my letters so that you will get them the soonest, for if you are [as] anxious to hear from me as I am from you, you wil not want the letters to wander about verey mutch before you get them. From your afectionate worser half, Wm. Winters

if you go to riseing sun, just tell them that they can write just as often and just as mutch as they please, and I will try not to get mad about it, for I can write to a few more corespondents like the ones I have now and not be kept verey busey at that as they only write, I guess, when they have nothing else to do and dont know what else to busey themselves at and they [remainder of letter illegible].

Sunday, January 17th, In camp at
Point Cavallo, Texas, 1864
Mrs. H. J. Winters
Dear wife, to day is the Sabath and the 17th day of 64 away down south in Texas and in the land of dixie, 21 hundred and 50 miles from Hope, Bartholomew County, Indiana,[6] a place, if my memory serves

me right, where a cross eyed buty [beauty] that I used to know lived last fall and who I hope for my own sake is there still, for I have a strong notion of comeing up there to see her again one of these days, if nothing hapens, after we have got this litle job of straightening up these texas rangers all fixed up. and we dont expect to be verey long at it you know, and then we will take a tour north if it is not objected to by uncle abe, as we canot think of doing any thing that our old uncle dont want us to, you know, for we have great respect for the old man, and as good obedient sons, we of course obey him in all he says we shall do. but we will soon be of age, and then we can act as we like for awhile, the old man says, and us boys have made up our minds that as soon as we are our own men we will come straight to the hoosier state and take the town of hope by storm or some other way. Now I dont want to frighten you, for we dont mean to take the town away but just make the inhabitants surender the privelege of the streets to us for the sake of having us come into it and increase the population by making the number of its inhabitants larger, which of course the town council will not object to in the least. Or if they do, it will be all the same, as we have come to the conclusion that we are able to take and hold any place we see fit, and after our old uncle gives us our papers we will be very apt to think just as we do now and act acordingly and make hope endure the presence of a few more of the linclonites [Lincolnites] no matter who of what company or Regiment he is from, for we are all alike: death on coffee beans, hard tack, and sow belly.

Well, hat, we are still the unwelcome ocupants of this sand neck and have no idea how long we shall be forced to disgrace this miserable piece of sand, but we will be apt to make it our abode and resting place untill we se[e] fit to remove our yankee carcasses to some other point to trouble the rebel texicans with our acquaintance for a while and learn them a few of rules of old abes house hold up north. And we are in hopes that they will not get made [mad] about it and go to kicking up a row, or we shall be put to the trouble of teaching them the laws of Abraham and let them know how the people do at other places down south, and that is do the best they can for something to eat until we see fit to give them a few hard tacks. And I think by that time they will

conclude that a yankey is about as good as a rebel if not a litle better.
we all think a good deal better, if not more than that, but the people
have not been away from home far for a good while, I think, and of
course cant have had any chance to find out what kind of a set of boys
our uncle has raised. But if they will think that they will get pretty well
acquainted with us and find out that we are not a bad set if they will
only let us have our own way. But if the[y] dont, why we will eat all the
sheep, cattle, and chickens there is in texas, if we can find them, and if
they have got any thing in the shape of preserves or honey, it will not
make the boys sick a bit to eat a very litle of it, say, about as mutch as
the[y] can conveniently.

Well, Hat, to day is as fine as a sumer day at home. the sun shines
warm, and the brease from the bay is very mild and pleasant, and we
are loling around our tents in the shade watching the tide as it comes
rushing toward the shore and listening to the breakers as they break
upon the sand and go back to come up in another vain atempt to
break over the sandy shore in their made career. It is a butifull day, and
I sit here and look at the gulf and think of home, and then I wish—but
it is a vain wish, for still I am here on this far of[f] distant shore but
still hopeing that this will not be always, and then to me it will not be
naught but the dull old gulfs continued roar but the voice of Home
and my litle ones. but it must be yet many days before that time may
arive, if indeed it ever does.

But we expect but litle fighting in texas, and our division expects to
be left here to garison this place, as it will bee our base of suplies untill
galveston is taken and that may be for some time to come.[7] I should
mutch rather remain here than to go back into the interior of the state,
as it is verey healthy here and must be mutch more pleasant in the
sumer time than it is back from the gulf coast, as the constant sea
breese make the coast a great deal more pleasent in the sumer time.
but how long we will stay here is more than I know or where we will
go to from here is more than I can tell. Our boys are all back at Algiers
and New Orleans, and some five or six of our company are exchanged. They are all well and expect to stay there untill they are all
exchanged, and if they do then they will have a good time of it, I think,

as they can have just as good a time there as they want. But we would like to have them with us [next line illegible] work to do as if we had a full Regiment and there is so few of us that it comes pretty tough the most of the time. and our Division is all that is here now, and we have all the picket duty and unloading of vesels to do, and if the other boys of our and the other Regiments was with us, it would not be near as bad. But we have to stand it.

I supose that cap[tain] Friedly and Hen Shults have got home and the time for recruiting is passed, and as far as we have heard have not got a single recruit, and so I supose that the draft must come off in Haw creek township. Now we are all anxious to know who is the lucky man in hope [Hope, Indiana] and want you to write as soon as the draft comes of[f], so that we can hear as quick as posible who is the man that drew a prize in the great lotery, for there must certainly be one luckey man in hope, if not more, and I want to know who he is.

We received a mail yesterday but not a scratch of a pen for me, and I was verey mutch disapointed indeed, as I felt certain that I would get several letters, as I got none in the mail before. So we have had two now and no news for me, but I hope for better luck when the next one arives, for I am in a dreadfull hurey to hear from you and the litle ones and the rest of the friends and to hear what the news is at home and to hear how you are all getting along. We are all well and hope that this will find you and all the friends the same. Give my love to all and put them in mind of writeing often.

From your afectionate
husband, William Winters


In Camp at Point Cavallo, 1864
Texas, Jan. 29th
Mrs. H. J. Winters
Dear wife, I received yours and Wesleys last on day before yesterday and have been so busey ever since that I could not answer it sooner.

We had just come back from a heavey march, and I was tired, sore, and worn out and had to go to work straightening up our camp and have been verey busey ever since. When I came back from our scout, my feet were worn out so that they bled, and I was chafed and galded [galled] and in an awfull fix. But I am about all right again now. We went up this point some fifty two miles on a reconoicence and compell the rebs up there to fight but they refused to do it, and we did not want them to as all we wanted was to find out what we could, and we done that and then come back to camp again just about as tired a sett of fellows as you ever saw.[8]

and then we are once more in camp and expecting to leave before maney days, but where to is more than I know. Some say we are to go to brownsville [Texas] and some say to indianola up here on the bay some twenty miles from here but I cant tell. But this mutch is certain—I think that we will move from here before you get this, but you direct to New Orleans as usual and your letters will follow us as they have done so far. We found Lieut Akin, Thomas Eaton, and five others of our company that were exchanged. They say that the rebs all own up that they are whiped and could not fight us, but some of them said that they were going to fight as long as they lived, but you know that such talk is all gamon, for they will do just as we would if we were in the same fix. We would quit after awhile, and so will they, for I dont think that they are aney fonder of being shot at than we are, and I know that most of our boys have seen as mutch of that as they want to and are ready to quit if the rebs will only just say the word, and we dont care how quick they say it, at least I dont, for I had a good deal rather come home than to stay down here in this miserable sandy desert for I am so confounded full of sand that I cant hardly keep my skin whole for the dam stuff rubing me when ever my cloths touch me, but I think that I shall have the good luck to live through the whole of it and get back safe and sound.

The wether is hot, and the grass is beginning to spring up green and butifull and looks and feels spring like indeed. The boys are all well and in the best of spirits and ready to go ahead and get this thing setled up so that they can get home once more, and I am in as big a hurey as aney of them, for I am anxious to get home again, for I am and always have been tired of this kind of a life, for to me it has no charmes at all. When we went up the point we got near enough to the main land to see timber and you would have thought that we were a lot of little boys if you had of seen us streach our necks and stand and look at the woods 8 or 9 miles of[f] but to us it was quite a sight.[9] we got some sweet potatoes, chickens, corn, and Beef. But we had a hard march of it, as we marched over one hundred miles in four days and a half and the sand got into our shoes and wore out the tops of our toes and the soles of our feet so that we could scarcely walk atall.

Hopeing that this will find you all well, I will have to stop for to day but will write again in a day or two. from

yours as ever, Wm Winters

In Camp at Point, Texas
Jan. 29th, 1864[10]
Mrs. H. J. Winters
Dear wife, I received a letter from you on last evening late dated Jan 7th just as you was starting for riseing sun, and I was verey glad to hear from you and that you and our litle girls were well. It was late last night when I received yours or I would of answered it at once. but to day will have to do for this time.

you wrote that you had received the money that I sent you. I am verey glad that you have got it at last for I and [had] begun to get uneasey about it. I have not been paid of[f] since that time, and I cant tell when we will be paid again or wether I shall be when I can send it home or not. But I hope that we will be where we can send our money home as quick as we draw it, for we all know that our families need it all. But you will have to make out the best you can untill that time, for I have only two cents to me name.

Well, I have just been out and got Lewis Hine[11] to shave me and shingle my hair, and it makes me look funey. But I feel a good deal better for it, as warm as it is here just now. We have had verey warm wether here now for over a week, and the grass begins to look quite green, and everey thing looks spring and pleasent. But it is rather to[o] warm for comfort during the day but quite pleasent at night. The citizens say that it is time that they had their gardens all made and corn planted. Now what do you think of that? at home while you are shivering around the fire we are laying around in our shirt sleeves.

We are having a fine time of it now, not having mutch to do for several days past, but how long this state of things will continue is more than I have aney means of knowing. But we dont expect it will last for verey long, for our brigade always has to do everything that is done and always has had to do it ever since we have been in the service, and we expect to have it to do as long as we are in the field.

But I hope that this thing will play out before a great while, for I cant see how the rebs can hold out in the[ir] condition. the boys say that the rebs that they saw while they were prisoners all owned that they were whiped and that they had no hope of ever gaining their independence at all. But they must yield after awhile, as they cant hold out always on nothing and for nothing. But enough of that. we are here, and the thing is not settled yet, and we cant get home, and so we will have to endure it the best way we can for a while longer and take a bigger spludge when we do get home.

we are all well and in good spirits and redy to whip any lot of rebs of the same number. Now I want you to tell Olivers folks if they see fit they can write a[s] often as they please, as it will not hurt my feelings at all to hear from them at aney time, for it is so seldom that we get aney news here, that we dont know aney thing about what is going on at all outside of our own armey here, and we are doing nothing here at present. But if we go up this point here we will probably have seen another bloody field before you get this. Give my love and respects to all and write soon.

from your afectionate
husband, Wm. Winters

In Camp at Point
Cavallo, Texas
Feb. 5th, 1864
Mrs. H. J. Winters
Dear wife, I just received yours written at Riseing Sun, also Nancys and one from Robert, and you may depend upon it I was hugely

tickled and unendingly glad to hear from you all once more. but I cant complain about not getting letters, as I have received five in the last two weeks, and that is doing remarkbly well in the army.

I am verey sorey to hear that the weather is and has been so extreemly cold. But I hope that you did not suffer with it as I did on the night that I wrote to you about that [march] we took on a sheep hunt up this desert of sand. But the thing has changed here since then, and it is warm and pleasant here now the most of the time and to[o] warm for comfort some times during the midle of the day. we have plenty of flies, spiders, and every other kind of creeping thing that is in the world I know, and then we have some other things that creep that you have not got at home, and that is rattle snakes in a bundance. I have seen eight since I have been here, and I havent seen the fourth of what has been killed here since we landed on this miserable neck of sand. I am a going to try to get the rattles from one and send them to you in a letter so that you can see what they look like. If I send one, you ned not be afraid of them, as they are perfectly harmless but quite a curiosity.

Well, some of our boys went a fishing with our major this afternoon and got a big mess of five large fish. we have a sane [seine] here that we captured from the old citizen that lives here, and we use it turn about, and the way we root the fish out is a caution to hoosiers. And they aford us a feast among our hard tack and old beef, for we get but litle hog now. The most of our meat rations is corns beef that was put up for old Noah when he went into the ark, for it sometimes smells loud enough to be heard a thousand yards of[f] hand, but a fellow can get used to aney thing when he is compelled to, and I have got used to so mutch that I dont know what I could not live on now. I think that all the single men in the field will be able to keep batchelors hall when they get out of the army, and if we stay here a great while we shall all be afraid of a woman if we ever get where there are aney again, for what few white women I have seen since I have been in texas look more like digger indians than they do like what they are intended to represent, and as greasey and dirty as a soap boiler.

Well, I guess I shall soon get this full, and it is getting along towards roll call, and I shall have to turn out to that or get a black mark and go on extra duty tomorow for it, and I dont want to do that, you know. Well, there the drumers are beginning to beat the call, and I must turn out or take the consequence. but I will keep on as long as I can, for I want to fill this sheet to night if I dont say verey mutch in it. it is as dark as pitch, and the gulf roars as if it was trying to get beyond its bounds.

Well, I have been out to roll call and said here, and now I shall have to quit for to night and fill another sheet tomorow if nothing hapens so that you are safe and enjoying your self. I will spread our blankets for the night and think of you as I go to sleep. Bill

Saturday, Feb. 6th, 1864
Point Cavallo, Texas

Well, Mrs. Hattie Jane, we have all just come in from grand review before the august persons of Maj. Generals Ord[12] and Daney[13] and Brig. General Ransom and a cavalcade of aids and staff officers, and I feel considerably releived since I have got my knapsack, haversack, canteen, and acouterments of[f], for you must know that we have to go out with every thing on our backs that we have got when we go on a grand review before our big folks no matter how wild it makes a man to stand up in line like a statue for four or five hours at a time. but we have got to go through with all of these things, you know, so that these big men can see what we look like. Well, we can do it all and then whip as many rebels as they choose to put before us if they will come out and fight like honerable soldiers, but that they wont do so we will have to chase and catch them the best way we can, but I confidently believe that the thing is about played out so far as hard fighting is concerned in this department, for all the prisoners that we have taken so far here all tell the same tale, and that is that the texican soldiers dont want to fight aney longer, as they all believe that we are just beginning to get our armey to work together, and then they say, "only look you have the most men in the field now and you are just bringing out three hundred thousand more," and the south cant do it as they have all their available force out now that they can get out. now, I think it is but reasonable to conclude that the thing is dying as fast as it can, and all their is to do now we all think is for the potomac army to take Richmond, and the work is done, for they canot hold aney other point the way they have that, but time alone can tell how the close of the war will be brought about, but I have no feers of our setling the business this sumer.

Well, I have eat my dinner of boiled beans and corn beef, and now I will finish this to you and get it of[f] as soon as posible. It is quite windy to day, and the way the sand drifts before it is funey, and then a fellow has to keep the side of his head towards it or his eyes will be full so quick that he cant tell where he is a going to. I have not had an oportunity of sending my box of shells home yet, but I am a going to send them if posible before we leave here. the last two or three letters I wrote to you I put several small shells into them for you and my litle girls. I have the bigest crabs claw that you ever saw, I know, and then I have one other curioisity to you, and that is a sea hog or a hog fish, as they are generaly called. Well, if I can get the things home that I have got, I think that there is a number of things that you never saw, but I did not pick them up so mutch for our gratifacation as I did for my litle girls, and I would give a months wages to be there when the box is opened if I can get it home, for I know that there will be some big capers cut over the shells and curious fish that I have put in it, but we may be ordered away from here before I get it of[f] and that will spoil all of my anticipated enjoyment with them and their shells.

Now, I guess that this will do for this time. I want you to stay at olivers just as long as you see fit and then go home or aney other place where you can pass of[f] the time the best until spring. this leaves me in the best of health and hope that it may arive safe and find you and all the friends well. I remain as ever yours,

Wm. Winters

give my love and best respects to all and tell them that I shall be verey glad to hear from that at aney time they wish to write and as mutch as they can find to write about. Bill

In Camp at Point
Cavallo, Texas

Mrs. H. J. Winters, Feb. 14th, 1864

Dear wife, I have just received a letter from you and Mrs. Sallie Holmes, both written on the same sheet of paper, and I was verey glad to hear from you and her and all the rest of the friends and that they are all well but verey sorey to hear that you were so unhappy and so mutch down in the mouth as sallie says. Now, you must not be the least uneasey about me, for this litle squable that we are fixing up now will soon be over with, and then I shall be free once more. and I think that the quickest route I can get home on will be the route that I shall take no matter where I am at the time I am discharged, for I am almost tired of being where I cant see a white woman and in an awfull way to see you and my litle girls. I am sorey that you had so mutch bad luck in going to Riseing sun, but I am glad to hear that you have got it again. now I want you to brighten up and try to pass of[f] the time and enjoy yourself as mutch as you can untill I get home again, and then we will fix the thing all up again and forget that I ever was away among the rebel states so long. And then I can tell you all about where I have been and what I have seen in the suney south and in the land of dixie, especialy since I have been on this side of the gulf of Mexico. Our time will soon be wearing off the last half of the time, as the 20[th] of this month we will have been out 18 months, and the other will soon pass away if we are not discharged before that time, which I confidently believe we will be, and I have no fears but what I shall get home all right safe and sound before the three years is out. so now I want you to keep your spirits up and not get the blues just because I am not at home, as I am in the best of health and fuley expect to get home in the course of the preasent year.

I have got two litle small envelopes, and I am going to write a litle letter to Edith and May and put in some litle small shells and send them in this to you, and you must read them to them and then write me all the particulars of the proceeding and what they say about pa and the letters. To day is St. Valentines day, but I have not seen aney Valentines. If I could get aney I would send a few home, but we are in a part of the world where I think that such a thing as a valentine was never heard of before us yankey vandals came here to distrub the peace and quiet of the sons and daughters of the suney South. So you and all the rest will get no valentines from me this time. tell Nan and Sallie that I am verey thankfull for their falling in love with my photo but would be still more flatered if they had fell in love with me.

well, to day is a butiful one, bright and butifull, and the birds are chirping their litle songs and flying about as if they were as hapey as Kings.

I expect that we will leave this point tomorow or the day after, as we are under marching orders. but I cant say where to but that need make no diferance to your writeing. Direct as usual, and they will folow on after us sooner or later.

Well, I must write to sallie and to my two litle pets and send you all a litle shell apeice. We have not been paid yet. We are expecting to be paid next week if we do not move from here, but if we do there is no telling when we will get our money. But as this month is so near out, I had mutch rather that they would not pay us until next month, for then they will owe us four months pay, and I had a good deal rather get 68 dollars than 34. But we have to take it as we can get it and make no remarks.

Give my love and respects to all the friends and write soon from yours afectionately,
Wm. Winters
to my wife

The following letters were enclosed with the above, for Winters's children.

Miss E. A. Winters
Well Miss edith, how do you do? and how do you like your visit at uncle olivers? I guess you and May and your cousins are having a fine time of it and telling each other about a great maney things. well, pa

wants you to be good girls and study and try to learn as fast as you can so when I come home you can read to me about the war and tell me all about your visits and what you saw in cincinnati and Riseing Sun.

now, I want you to look at these litle shells that I have put in this for you and then give them to ma to keep for you so you will not loose them, for pa went down on the beach and picked them up for his litle daugheters. Kiss mama for pa and be good girls.

From your afectionate,

father

Miss E. M. Winters

Well, May, what do you think about you[r] shells? Are they not real pretty litle funey fellows? Pa wants you to show them to all your cousins and tell them that they was picked up on matagorda bay by your pa, and when ma writes again to pa you must tell her what to write for you so that pa will hear all about how you like you[r] uncle and aunt English and how you like to ride on the cars and a whole lot. Tell ma to write to pa and kiss her for me and be a good litle girl, and when pa comes home he will by you a nice big [illegible]. From papa to his litle daughter

May Winter

# EIGHT

# "When I Come Home Again"

In March 1863 Maj. Gen. Nathaniel P. Banks launched an expedition up the Red River, across the state of Louisiana, and toward Texas beyond. Among the substantial force that composed this expedition was the Thirteenth Corps, including Winters's own Sixty-seventh Indiana.

The march once again took Winters through a new area of the exotic South, a very inviting one in its enticing spring livery and after the bleak sands of the Matagorda Peninsula. He liked the look of the land, enjoyed the weather, and even went so far as to opine, "I would like to live here verey mutch if it was not cursed with rebels and slaverey." Still, "as it is, I think that my hoosier home is far the best, and I wish that I was agoing to start for it tomorow."

Home was never far from his thoughts, and he asked Hattie to tell Edith and May that "pa thinks of them every time he sees litle girls playing in the yards or looking at us as we march by." He thought of Hattie too. He had her picture with him, and of it he said, "I often look at it and think of home."

He sometimes mentioned the dangers that lay ahead, but he expressed a consistent—if not quite absolute—confidence that he would survive. "I have an idea in my head that I shall get through all safe and sound," he wrote, "at least I hope so." He looked forward to returning to his trade as a saddle and harness maker and admonished Hattie, "If my tools are rusting, I wish you would get them and keep them dry if you can, for I may want to use them again one of these days." Camped in Natchitoches, Louisiana, as the army prepared to move out for the final leg of the advance to Shreveport, he wrote, "We will be at Shrevesport before you receive this and it may be in eternity, some of us, but we are all in the best of spirits and health . . . and ready for all that is our duty to do as soldiers and hope to have the pleasure of seeing our homes, friends, and dear ones after our trials and deprivations are over and this cruel war is at an end."

꜠

In Camp at Berwick City,
Louisiana,[1] Feb. 28th, 1864
Mrs. H. J. Winters

Dear wife, we arived here on yesterday about two oclock, two days and three nights from Point Cavallo, Texas. We did not come by New Orleans or I should have written to you from there. seven companies of our Regiment left us at Cavallo and arived here some three days before we did. They came around by the way of New orleans. We came by the way of chafalia bay and chafalia River to Berwick bay[2] and up the bay to our preasant camp on the oposite side of the bay from Bras[h]ear city. You of cours will say, what in the world have you come back to where you was a while before you went to texas? Well now, I cant tell you any thing about what we went to texas for and then come back here again. all I know is that we had a voige [voyage] of over a thousand miles and see a piece of what is said to be texas and had the fun of picking up a lot of shells that I shall express to you tomorow. And I want you to wash them all off nice and clean with a brush and give Mary Jane and vine some of them and after you have satisfied yourself with looking at the sea horse and sea hog and horny fish and a slime fish that I send with them I want you to let Dr. Stoss have the four fish as curiosities in the store, but tell him that I want him to save them. The shells you must keep among you, as I want to see them when I come home again.

we were mustered for pay again to day and expect to be paid in the cours of a few days. I was in hopes that we would be paid off here, but we are ordered to be ready to march tomorow. We go from here to franklin, some 80 miles up bayou tesh,[3] and from there we expect to go with an expedition against Alexandria and Shrevesport in this state. I think that we will stop at Franklin untill all the troops get together, and I think that we will get our pay there. I hope so for your sake, for I know how badly you need it. if we get our four months pay there, I will send you all that I can spare as quick as we get it, but if we dont get it, hat, you will have to make out the best way you can untill I can send you money. I know that it greives you to be out of money, and I feel as sory for you and our litle girls as you can for me, but we will have to endure it until this cursed rebelion is put down, which I think will certinly be during the preasant year. you must do as you think best for yourself and the children. After this pay day I shall be abel to send you about 30 dollars for everey two months pay, as after this time I will not have any transportation to pay. My fare from home to New orleans had to come out of my pay this time, and that will cut it some fourteen dollars, but if we are paid for four months I will send you some 45 or 50 dollars.

We had a butifull trip across the gulf. it was as still and smooth as the ohio river.

Yes, I must tell you this makes the fourth letter that I have written to day, one to Bell, one to wes, and one to E. J. Porter. I got one from each one of them when I landed here on yesterday afternoon, and I answered them all today and am writing this to you for fear that I will not get the chance tomorow. The box of shells that I am a going to express tomorow has a partition in it and two letters, one for you and the other for charley bannes wife. The shells in the bigest part of the box are yours. You will find a bottle in your side of the box, and you can give her hers and keep your own, and you will have [remainder of letter missing].

In camp at Berwick City
March 4th, 1864
Mrs. H. J. Winters

Dear wife, I received a letter from you this morning written at home, and I was glad to hear from you and that you and the children were well, but was very sorey that the hogs eat all your apples for you.

This is the second letter that I have written to you from this place since we have been here, but when I wrote the other I did not expect that we would be here now. But here we are yet but expect to leave in a day or two. but we may stay here a month for all that I can tell. I hope for your sake that we will stay here until we are paid off, but if we are ordered away, why, of course I cant help it but must obey, but I hope for the best.

The weather is butifull and evereything is putting forth and the air is already fragrent with the smell of wild flowers. We are not doing any duty now of aney consequence, and the boys—the most of them—busey themselves cutting trees and killing coons just back of our camp, and one of co. D boys cut a bee tree to day and got two buckets of honey. There is a large force of cavalry comeing throug from New Orleans to go out on the expedition with us, so if we hapen to get into another snap like the boys did at carion crow, we will have cavalry to help the rebel cavalry to do their duty. but enough of this.

I expressed a box of shell to you the other day. you will no doubt get it before you do this, and you must do with the shells that you dont want to keep as you please of cours. Only keep a good lot of them for my pets. If you get the box, tell Edith and May that pa says they must keep their slates until they are big girls, and so pa can help them cipher on them when I get home again.

you wanted to know if I could read your writeing. Yes, I can read it, and all that I got to say [is that] you dont write half enough when you do write. Now, the more you write, the better, as you will not only please me, but you will improve your handwriting the more. well, I am tired of writeing. I have been helping make out pay rolls, receipt rolls, and a lot of other company writeing, and I havent had a pen out of my hand since yesterday morning, only when I eat and slept.

I put into this a ring with a pearl set in it that I made, while I was in texas, out of a rubber buton. I think that it will just fit your third finger. I guess you will think I was in a hurey, for I comenced this [letter] on the wrong side [of the paper]. If we leve here before I get another letter from home, I will try and write to let you know where we are a going to if I can find out when we leave. Give my love to all and kiss my babies for me.

from you afectnate Husband,
William Winters

In Camp at Hardins
plantation, La.
Mrs. H. J. Winters, March 11, 1864

Dear wife, I received a letter from you last night at 12 oclock and got up and read it as soon as I received. I am very glad to hear that you are all well and that you got one of the letters that I sent with shells in them. And here I will ask, did you get the letter that I driected to riseing Sun for you with two litle letters in it with some small shells in them for you and my litle girls? When you write again, tell me wether you receive it or not.

Well, hat, you can see by the heading of this that we are once more on the move. We are now encamped on a plantation about five miles above franklin on what they call bayou tesh.[4] we are waitting for some more troops to come up, and then we shall move forward again. we expect to go over the same ground that our forces went over last fall, when our regiment were all captured, and from there to Alexandria and Shrevesport. At least that is what we expect at the present, but we may be badly mistaken about all of it, but I think not.

Well, we have not been paid of[f] yet, and I cant tell when you will get any money. But I hope that we will get our money while we are here, for I know that you need it badly, for your have not got aney for so long. But, mama, I cant help it, for I cant compell them to pay me. but this mutch I can do: if I live to get out of this, they will not get me in again, for the longer a man is in the service, the worse he is used. But enough of that.

the mail goes out in a few minutes, and I want to get this started, so you will have to put up with the shortest letter that I have ever written to you since I was at home.

this is a lovely country here, me, all flowers and shrubrey, and the musick of the mocking birds make the day mulodious with their songs. I got some flower almonds as I come along, and I send you several in this. I am well. Give my love to all and write soon.

From yours as ever

William Winters

Burns Plantation, La., March 12th, 1864

Mrs. H. J. Winters

Dear wife, I have just received a letter from you dated feb. 20th [in response to the letter] that I directed to Riseing Sun. well, there is one more due you that I directed to the same place with two little letters in it for our litle girls. I wrote to you all about it in my last from this place the next day after we arived here. I called it Hardins plantation then, but I was mistaken in the name.

Well, the wind blows so that I can hardly write at all, but I am afraid that will have to write, so I will do the best I can, and you will have to make it out the best you can. The weather is hot, and everey thing is growing as fine as can bee. The trees are all as green as in full sumer. I saw some butifull flower gardins as we marched through franklin the other day, and I thought how my litle girls would like to have been there to pluck them and look at the shells along the walks, but that cant be. They must wait untill the winter is over in their northern home before they can see aney flowers, while here they bloom out in the open air all winter. This is a butifull country down here, and I would like to live here verey mutch if it was not cursed with rebels and slaverey. But as it is, I think that my hoosier home is far the best, and I wish that I was agoing to start for it tomorow instead of starting to try to kill my fellow men. But that is our mision now, and we must fullfill it if we get shot in the undertaking.

Our cavalry pickets had a litle skirmish with some Reb cavalrey on yesterday but nobody hurt. So you see that there is some of the whelps are watching us, but we dont expect to have aney fighting to do before we get to alexandria or in that vacinity some where. But that may be before you receive this, but I have no desire to see an other reb in arms while I live, but I shall be compelled to do it, I recon. But I have an idea in my head that I shall get through all safe and sound, at least I hope so.

I sent you some flowerey almonds in my last that I picked as I was marching along. We have not been paid of[f] yet, and I dont know when we will be either, but I do hope that it will [not] be long for I have no more paper or envelopes or money, and I often think of you and my pets and how badly you need it. but it cant bee helped, for the government seems to have forgotten all but the vetrans and people at home the same way, for it seems that they cant offer big enough bounties to them, while us devils have to look on an wait.[5] but we hope that there will be a time when we can put them in mind of what they promised to do when we come out. but never a dollar has been paid that we have heard of. Yet Bartholamew county was to pay 22 hundred dollars among the families of the men that went out in the first three cals, but we have not heard of a dollar being paid yet. Well, that makes no diferance. They have got us fast, and now they must pay some body else to come out to save their own hides. But I think that it will all come around after awhile. Now, Hat, you will have to do the best that you can, and as soon as I draw, I will send you everey cent that I can.

If my tools are rusting, I wish you would get them and keep them dry if you can, for I may want to use them again one of these days. I heard to day that some of the recruits for our company are at New orleans. Tell vine that I received a paper from her to day with a note inside all right and will anser it tomorow if we do not move to[o] soon in the morning. Send me word about the box of shells as soon as you get them, if you have not before you get this. You must excuse the writeing, for I know that it is bad, but the wind is the fault of it.

we have great times making tafy out of sugar and molases. My health is all right, and I would give a bushell to be at home with you to night. Give my love to all and write soon. yours as ever,

Wm. Winters

What do you think of the ring I sent you in my last?

In Camp at Burns

plantation, La.

Mrs. H. J. Winters, March 15th, 1864

Dear wife, I will take the advantage of a favorable oportunity to send you a few lines that you may have some idea of our whereabouts. We are on the same old camp ground that we were when I wrote last. I thought that we would not be here then, but here we are, but we canot remain here but a few days longer, as the army here is all in motion but our core, and of course we canot expect to stay behind. The road has been crowded with troops passing us for the last three days, and [we] expect to start in a day or two. I never saw so many cavalry in my life as I saw for the last two days. But I think that we need a few more infantry, but perhaps these generals know how maney men they do want. Two negro regiments passed us this forenoon, and I understand that there is some more behind. I had mutch rather see one of them shot than a white man.

the weather is fine to day, is cool and pleasant. The roads are verey dusty, and it is agoing to be very disagreeable marching, but I had rather have a litle dust than mud. The boys are having a big time pulling taffy all day long. As soon as they eat their breakfast some one comences to boil some sugar and molasses, and then it is kept up all day. a good maney of the boys are cooking pepper grass greens, and some are out hunting poke weed and mustard for greens, and some are pitching horse shoes, aney thing to pass of[f] the time. we got a mail since I wrote to you last, and I felt certain that I would get a letter from somebody, but nara letter for Bill. But then I dont expect one everey mail, but how long it will be after we leave here before we get another is more than I can tell, but I hope that it will not be long. But, Hat, I must tell you that if you donot get a letter from me for some time after this one, you must not think strange or hard of it, for I dont know how we will be provided for in the way of mails after we get back into the interior of the state, but I hope that we will have a chance to send a letter once a week, but we may not have for a month, and then I am out of paper and envelopes and no chance to get aney and of cours cant write as often as I have been doing here to fore. so if you dont get quite as maney [letters], dont get woried about it, for I will write as often as I can get the chance while on the march, and I want you to write as often if I dont, for yours will follow us up, and if we dont get them often then I will get the more when they do come.

I send this by Lieut. Friedly. he has resigned[6] and will start for home tonight or tomorow and will bring you this, so you can ask him all the questions that you want about how I am standing it.

tell edith and may that pa wants them to be good girls and love ma and learn to read and write on those two slates that I sent them. Tell them pa thinks of them every time he sees litle girls playing in the yards or looking at us as we march by. Kiss them for me and tell me in your next wether you got the shells and slates or not. Give my love to all and write often. From yours as ever,

Wm. Winters

I send a letter with this for Bell. Bill


in camp near Alexandria,

Louisiana

March 27th, 1864

Mrs. H. J. Winters

Dear wife, We arived here on yesterday and received a mail, and I had the pleasure of receiving a letter from you, and you may be certain we were a happy set of fellows. I was glad to hear from you and that you were well. We were on the march from franklin to this place 10 days. And tired enough but we had no trouble on the march and all went of[f] merily. You have read all about the capture of this place before we got here, so I cant write any thing new about that. the place is a nice thriveing looking place on the bank of Red river. The country that we marched over from Berwick to this place is I think one of the richest that I have ever saw and a great maney southern palaces adorn the road we have marched since leaveing Berwick about two hundred miles and are now just about half way to shrevesport, our place of destination, and we will no doubt be there before this reaches you, as we expect to start tomorow morning on the tramp again. the forces of Gen. A. J. Smith[7] that took this place before our arival will go with us, so if the rebs do conclude to fight there, we will have force enough to suround them as we did at Vicksburgh, but the opinion is that we will not get a fight out of them in this state, but if they intend to fight at all we had mutch rather have them stop and do it, as we dont like to chace them so far.

The boys are all well. Clint Neely and his Brother[8] and george Hansen[9] are with us. They come to us at franklin the night before we left. Charly Bannes got a letter from his brother informing him of the death of his two children with spotted fever. He takes it hard, and I pity him from my heart, for I know how it took me when I heard of our litle billys death, and it must be harder when we loose all. I have been uneasey ever since for fear that my other litle pets may be taken from us by some dreaded disease, and, ma, do take care of our litle ones, for I dont know what I would do if we loose another while I am away. But I know that you will do all you can for them. Well, hat, I guess that we will get some of our pay to day but not the half of what we aught to have. I am well and have been all the time and hope that I will remain so. well, hat, I am tired of writeing but not to you. I set up last night and wrote untill twelve and all this forenoon making out pay rolls and certifacates and I can [passage illegible] . . .

. . . for me and tell them that pa thinks of them often and wishes that he was at home to tell them all he has seen. Write soon. From yours,

Wm. Winter

What is orlando doing and how does he look?

I come verey near spoiling you photo on the march, as it was raining and I forgot it, but it is neerly as good as ever, and I often look at it and think of home. Bill

in camp at Nachitoches,
Louisiana, April 4th, 1864

Mrs. H. J. Winter

Dear wife, I just received six letters, and I almost jumped up and down when I got them into my hands. I am so glad to hear that you and the children are well, and I hope that you and they will not be visited with either of those fell diseases that is scourgeing the country, and, ma, oh, do take care of our litle girls, for I cant loose them.

We are in camp here and have been for a couple of days but are ready to be called out at any moment, for we have drove the enemy before us for several days before we halted, and they are waiting to engage us at Pleasant hill, some thirty five miles above us on the road to shreveport and expect to give us a whiping there, they say, but they have not got the men to do it with. But they will no doubt fight us there.

this place is quite a nice town with a large convent called the Sacred heart of Jesus. There is quite a number of nuns and children that are put here to go to school for fear of the influences of hereticks. I was through a grave yard of theirs with tom Eaton and picked some myrtle flowers, and I will put them in this. The country here and between here and Alexandria is considerably hilley and rolling and covered with pitch pine, and as we marched through it I thought of the pine clad hills of my boyhood home and how oft I had rambled through them in chaseing the nimble squirrill and rabbit, and then I thought of my own litle ones, and a tear of sorow stole down my cheek that I turned aside and wiped away. The country is lovly and rich but mostly catholic. The town of Nachitoches is situated on what they call old river or old red river, the bed of what is red river proper, but the river runs some four miles from here now through a new chanell.

We expect to go forward in a day or two and are liable to be sent at any time. we have not been paid of[f] yet, and I canot tell when we will be paid.

I got a letter from wes. He seems to think that lando might of given more than he did and Jim a litle less, but I guess he is not following a verey honorable calling, or he would not have quite so mutch mony to spend as he apears to have. I got a letter from Bell and one from Mary Jane. Wes wrote that he was agoing to sell out his furniture and move back to the gate and keep house for Aleck. All good enough. vine wrote that she was agoing to the city to keep house for Jim awhile. From what was wrote, Aus and his wife have both joined christy chappell, a blessing to his family if he will only stick to it.

well, hat, we have about a hundred miles more to march to shreveport, and perhaps we may have a couple of fights before we get there, but I hope not, but if we do we will be at Shrevesport before you receive this and it may be in eternity, some of us, but we are all in the best of spirits and health and spirits and ready for all that is our duty to do as soldiers and hope to have the pleasure of seeing our homes, friends, and dear ones after our trials and deprivations are over and this cruel war is at an end.

The weather is butifull, and everything is growing and spreading its buties and oders to all, heeding not the preasence of an invading armey. Some of the fair ones of this country take pleasure in abuseing us in unmeasured terms for comeing into their country and homes and say that we had better stay at home and attend to our business and come to disgrace their homes with our yankey preasence. But we cant help what they think about us. We are all well. My own [health] is as good as it ever was in my life, and I hope that it may continue to be so for the balance of my term, if I am compeled to serve it out. well, hat, if I had the time I would write you more, if I had time to do so, but will have to conclude with this, as the mail goes out in a few minutes, and it may be the only chance to write before we get to Shreveport, and I would not miss sending this to you, as I know that you want to know where I am. Hopeing that this will find you all well, I remain yours as ever, William Winters

Two days later, April 6, 1864, Banks led his army onward from Natchitoches and nearby Grand Ecore for the last leg of its advance toward Shreveport. He managed the march miserably, placing his one thousand supply wagons where they would be most in the way and allowing his column to stretch out for more than twenty miles.

No sooner had the army taken the narrow road out of Grand Ecore, through what one Union trooper called "a howling wilderness" of red clay, sand, deep woods, and pine thickets, than the pace of the skirmishing at the front end of the column picked up appreciably. The Confederates obviously were present in some force just ahead, and their cavalry was getting downright saucy. Yet Banks ignored warnings from his cavalry commander and, on Franklin's advice, kept the cavalry's own three hundred supply wagons between the horse soldiers and the rest of the army. That meant that if the bluejacketed troopers ran into really serious opposition, they would be on their own for the first hour or two—the time it would take Federal infantry to move past the two or three miles of narrow road clogged with the cavalry's wagons.

On April 7 the fighting at the front of the column was almost continuous and sometimes pretty hot. At the repeated urging of his cavalry commander, Banks finally agreed at least to send a brigade of infantry up to support the cavalry. The recipient of Banks's order at about 10:30 that night was Col. W. J. Landram, commander of the Fourth Division of the Thirteenth Corps. He had two brigades, and he chose the first, that of William Winters and the Sixty-seventh Indiana. They were camped at Pleasant Hill, which they had reached late that afternoon after a twenty-mile march. The regimental historian recalled that it seemed they "had scarcely bivouacked for the night when" they were called into ranks again. The order directed the brigade to march at 3:00 A.M. in order to join the cavalry eight miles up the road by daylight, but the chronicler of the Sixty-seventh recalled that they "lay in line of battle" all night before moving out.[10]

They reached the cavalry just after daybreak, at about 6:30 A.M., April 8, and found the horse soldiers already stopped cold on the near edge of a stump-dotted clearing by tough Confederate resistance in the far treeline. The Twenty-third Wisconsin was in the lead, and the Sixty-seventh's Col. Frank Emerson, temporarily commanding the brigade, ordered them into line on the right of the road while he sent his own regiment, now temporarily under the command of Maj. Francis A. Sears of Bedford, Indiana, into line on the left. Together they swept forward past the dismounted cavalrymen. "And now," one of the Hoosiers recalled, "the ball opened pretty lively." The Rebels fought stubbornly, but a determined advance by the midwesterners, supported by some of the Union horse artillery, gradually pushed them back.[11]

This was to be the pattern for that long morning, the men beating their way through mile after mile of thicket, often under fire. "The timber on each side of the road was heavy and dense," Colonel Landram wrote, "which rendered it very difficult to move in line, and the marching was tedious and tiresome to the men, the enemy contesting every foot of the ground as we advanced." The Sixty-seventh's historian put it more colorfully. "Now the road here was extremely narrow, while the thick woods on either side were full of underbrush matted together by long green briers, making it almost impossible to move in line of battle, while the enemy fell back and took advantage of the best positions, from which they would pour a volley into our skirmish line, then drop back to another position and await our coming."[12]

Toward midday, about four miles from the point at which they had first made contact with the enemy, the Sixty-seventh turned over its share of the lead to the Seventy-seventh Illinois and got the respite of filing into the road for another two miles or so of relatively easy marching. Then it was back into line and into the brush again. "We continued skirmishing and working our way through this terrible jungle," one of them recalled, until about midafternoon. By that time they were about four miles short of the town of Mansfield, Louisiana. Ahead lay a broad, open field, eight hundred yards deep and twelve hundred from side to side. In the middle of it the ground rose gently but substantially to a ridge, and on the ridge Confederate skirmishers were visible. The Union cavalry commander, directing the advance guard, ordered Landram to drive the Rebels out of the field. Landram had his doubts but went ahead. To his surprise, the Confederates fell back as his men approached. The Federals took position behind a rail fence at the edge of the woods on the far side of the field. Ominously, however, Union skirmishers pressing deeper into the woods discovered not only Confederate cavalry but also infantry in line of battle.[13]

Confederate major general Richard Taylor had finally assembled a force with which he hoped to be able to stop Banks's advance. In all, he had about fifty-eight hundred infantry and three thousand cavalry. Behind the rail fence along the edge of the clearing, the Federals numbered only about twenty-four hundred infantry and about that many cavalry, even after the arrival of Landram's second brigade, which he had several times that morning requested permission to bring up in order to relive the exhausted men of the first. Now the second brigade simply went into line beside the first in the face of the new Confederate threat. There could be no further thought of advancing; the question now was whether they could hold their ground. Through most of the afternoon both sides waited, while skirmishing, sometimes intense, continued between the lines and on the flanks. Gen. Thomas E. G. Ransom, who had so impressed Winters and his comrades shortly after taking command back in January, arrived on the scene, and, sometime later, so did Banks, despite Franklin's assurance that nothing was amiss and no fighting imminent.[14]

Only a couple of hours of daylight remained when the waiting came to an abrupt, stomach-tightening end with the rising discordant yip-yipping of the Rebel yell coming through grass, trees, and brush in front and on both flanks. On the Federal left-center, its left flank on the road, was the Sixty-seventh Indiana. To its left, in the road itself, Capt. Ormand F. Nims's Second Massachusetts Battery roared to life, belching shell and canister at the onrushing Confederates. "Never before," wrote the Sixty-seventh's historian, "did we see a battery work harder, faster or more efectually than did Nims' battery at this moment—hurling grape and canister, and mowing great swaths through the lines of the advancing enemy." But the Rebels made good use of the available cover. Moving from behind "the timber and thickly matted underbrush, they were upon us before the ball opened," a Hoosier recalled.[15]

Every officer who saw the Sixty-seventh in action that day noted in his report the courage with which they fought.[16] At first it appeared they might stop the Confederates, but there were simply too many of the gray- and butternut-clad attackers. Banks had put his army in an impossible situation with its leading elements at the mercy of a force not one-third its total size. Now Landram's midwesterners, outnumbered by enemy infantry on the field of battle by a ratio of well over two to one, were going to have to pay the price.

On the left, south of the road, the dismounted cavalry gave way as overwhelming Confederate numbers swept around their flank. Then the Twenty-third Wisconsin could hang on no longer and broke for the rear. The victorious Rebels rushed toward Nims's battery, and the gunners scrambled to limber up. Lt. Warren K. Snow, the battery's second in command, dismounted to help and fell, mortally wounded. Other gunners went down. Nims and his remaining men got three of their guns away; neither time nor live horses remained for the other three. Yelling like fiends, the exultant Confederates swung the abandoned guns around and sent loads of canister hissing into the flank of the Sixty-seventh, cutting into the Hoosiers' ranks like a scythe through ripe wheat. General Ransom galloped along the line from the right, where the Federals were still holding, but any hopes that he could restore the situation on his left were snuffed out when he toppled from his horse, badly wounded. Colonel Emerson went down, and presently there was nothing more for the men of the Sixty-seventh to do but get away—those who still could. "It seemed like an act of providence that enabled us to escape across the field alive, though many did fall killed and wounded," wrote the regiment's chronicler. In fact, of the 2,413 Federal officers and men in action, 1,136 became casualties that day.[17]

The fighting raged on until nightfall, and by that time the other division of the Thirteenth Corps had also fought a lonely battle against the entire Confederate army and been defeated. The Rebel advance finally halted, partially because of darkness, partially because of the successful stand by a division of the Nineteenth Corps several miles back down the road, and partially because a large proportion of the Confederate soldiers had fallen out of ranks to revel in the abundance of supplies in the more than three hundred wagons they had captured. The wagons had so clogged the narrow road as to necessitate the abandonment of every gun of the several Union batteries that had taken part in the battle, including the three pieces Nims's men had brought off at such cost. The battle, known as Sabine Cross Roads or Mansfield, was the greatest Confederate victory west of the Mississippi.[18]

The list of killed and wounded of my command cannot be ascertained, inasmuch as the enemy retained possession of the field, but that we suffered severely there can be no doubt. Many brave men fell, but they fell with their faces to the foe. Honored be their memory.

Report of Col. William J. Landram, Commanding Fourth Division, Thirteenth Corps, of engagement at Sabine Cross Roads, Louisiana[19]

Back in Hope, Indiana, that spring, Hattie stopped receiving letters from her husband. After the letter written in Natchitoches April 4, in which he had expressed his hope "to have the pleasure of seeing our homes, friends, and dear ones after our trials and deprivations are over and this cruel war is at an end," no other letter came. By July she had begun to make inquiries that would go as far as would ever be possible toward confirming what she must surely by then have suspected. The letters below are replies to some of her inquiries and demonstrate, among other things, that Winters's company commander was far less literate than Winters had been. The punctuation, of course, has all been added.

Algiers, La
July 27th, 1864
Mrs. Winters

I received your kind favor of 14th inst. And hasten to answer its contents. I am very sorry you was keep in suspense, but I assure you that it was not my fault but the mail agents, as it must have been misplace. I would be far from keeping you or any other soldier wife in suspense, for I think it is my first duty to inform the friends an the wives of soldiers, which I did immedatly to all the nearest friends of miss[ing] members of Co. I, 67 Ind.

Sergt. Winters, Corp. Burk,[20] Tho. Gaither[21] & Geo. Shuck[22] was miss from Co. I. we received letters by flags of truce given the names of all prisoners in Texas that was captured out 67 Regt. out of that numbers was Burk & Gaither, Winters & Shuck names not being amongst them. We all so received a list of wound prisoners at Moorsfield, but none out of Co. I was in the list. So I cannot here any thing of him nor Shuck. If he is a live he must started and was left on the road sick. The prisoners that was exchange was captured last fall, none paroled in this department.

The best infermation I can git is that he was killed on the field of battle at Sabine Cross roads. Its hard to give up such a kind husband and father, but such is the sorrows of war. Winter was kind & good soldier and was well like by all the members of the compeny. Any infermation at any time I will gladly give in reffrnce to him. I remain as ever your friend

Wm. H. Aikin

To Mrs. Winters

Morganza, La.

Dec. 21 st, 1864

Mrs. Winters

I forwards the final statements of your husband Sergt. Wm. Winters, who was killed at Mansfield, La., on 8 day of April 1864.

We received notice from the *Editor of New Orleans Era* stating that a notice had been sent to him for publication, from you, indirectly stating that the company officers had fail to do there duty.

I have written you some three letters, given you all the infermation I could in reffernces to his death up to this time. I do not know whether he is dead, but I have made out his final settlement between him and the gov. The reglations of U.S. Gov says that the final statements shall not be made out unless an officers certificates is attach stating that he was kill. But I have made the certificate which settle it. I am allway willing to do any thing I can for any the members of my company and especialy Segt. Winters, who was my warmest friend. He was brave, true, & patriotic and well like by all that knew him. And when I should wrong such brave soldier wife as Sergt. Winters, I think I would commit and unpardnable sin.

Pay due him from 31st Oct. 1863 up to April 8th 1864 and seventy five dollars bounty [illegible]. You can git your pay by making application, as full settlement is made with the War Department at Washington, D. C.

Please write and state what you wrote to the Editor in Reffernce to Company officers of this company. I have tried to do my duty, and if I have fail to do my duty it has been through ignorance.

I remain your Friend

Wm. H. Aikin

To Mrs. Winters

P.S. I sent to my brother Elmer letters to hand to you. I have a pincushing of Winters that I will send you the first oppertunity.

W.H.A.

In an age before dog tags or any systematic, regular procedure for identifying and burying (much less repatriating) fallen soldiers, the uncertainty that must have plagued Hattie Winters was not rare. The most famous such case during the Civil War was that of Sgt. Amos Humiston, found dead on the battlefield of Gettysburg clutching a photograph of his three children. He was identified, and his family notified of his fate, only when reproductions of the photograph were published in the North and recognized by friends of the family.

After the war was over, Clara Barton, founder of the American Red Cross, headed an investigation into the matter of the graves of Northern war dead. She concluded that 315,555 such graves existed but that the occupants of 143,155—fully 45 percent— were unidentified. For a further 43,973 Union soldiers who had died during the conflict, no known graves existed.[23] William Winters fell into one of those two categories. No clue as to his fate ever found its way into official records.

Hattie Winters had to go on with her life and with raising her two little girls. That was no easy matter with the family's breadwinner gone. It was therefore of great importance to secure the small pension the government promised to soldiers' widows.

Office of Robert Denny,

Notary Public and Claim Agent,

Indianapolis, Ind., March 1st, 1866

Mrs. Hattie Winters

Hope, Ind.

Madam: I have this day received your Pension Certificate entitling you to Eight-Dollars per month since the 8th day of April 1864. It is dated February 23d, 1866 and is payable at Madison, Indiana, by M. Litton, Esq., Pension Agent. I thout it best to write to you before sending the Certificate, not knowing but you might be absent and there would be some risk of losing it. You will please call or send me my Fee which is $10.00 with directions how and where you wish the Certificate sent—whether by mail or Express—and I will give it immediate attention, as you may direct. Awaiting your reply I am

Respectfully &c.

Robert Denny

P.S. Should you at any time decide to do yourself the kindness to get married your Pension will cease the date of Marriage, but your children will be entitled to receive the same Pension in your stead till they are 16 years of age. Should it become necessary to have the Pension transferred to your children I hope you will not forget me, as I flatter myself I am as well prepared to do justice to Claimants as any man in the State. Should you decease, your children will be entitled to your pension.

Yours truly,

R. Denny

Hattie must have been suitably impressed with Robert Denny's preparation to do her justice, for on March 10, 1867, at Indianapolis, Indiana, she married him.

# NOTES

*Introduction*

1. For information on Winters's family and early life I have drawn on the holdings of the Bartholomew County (Indiana) Historical Society and the records of the 1860 census (p. 12), on microfilm in the holdings of the Columbus (Indiana) Public Library, as well as on the oral history passed down to living descendants of William Winters.

2. E. B. Long with Barbara Long, *The Civil War Day by Day: An Almanac, 1861–1865* (New York: Da Capo, 1971), 265; Richard Crawford, *The Civil War Songbook* (New York: Dover, 1977), vii.

3. R. B. Scott, *The History of the 67th Regiment Indiana Infantry Volunteers, War of the Rebellion* (Bedford IN: Herald Book and Job Printing, 1892), 5.

*1. "An Army amongst Them"*

1. Scott, *History of the 67th*, 1–6.

2. High bluffs line both banks of the Green River in this area, and Winters probably refers to one of the hills on the south bank, near the end of the railroad bridge. The railroad passed just west of town, and Munfordville would have been visible across the river to the northeast, while the smaller village of Woodsonville lay on the south bank directly to the east.

3. The late summer of 1862 was marked by a severe drought that had a significant effect on military operations between the Appalachians and the Mississippi.

4. Confederate colonel John Hunt Morgan specialized in daring cavalry raids that suited his love of high-stakes gambling. His summer 1862 raid into Kentucky was probably his most successful exploit. He tore up railroads and played

havoc with the supply system of Buell's army, disrupting its operations. James A. Ramage, *Rebel Raider: The Life of General John Hunt Morgan* (Lexington: University Press of Kentucky, 1986), 20–83; Thomas Lawrence Connelly, *Army of the Heartland: The Army of Tennessee, 1861–1862* (Baton Rouge: Louisiana State University Press, 1967), 194–95; James Lee McDonough, *War in Kentucky: From Shiloh to Perryville* (Knoxville: University of Tennessee Press, 1994), 55–60.

5. The distance from Munfordville to Glasgow is twenty-five miles by road, approximately nineteen as the crow flies. Neither Morgan nor any other Confederate was in Glasgow at the time, though Bragg's army would eventually advance through that town toward Munfordville.

6. Contrabands. Technically, the term referred to escaped slaves who had entered Union lines, but it came to be used—as in this case—for all blacks.

7. Frank Emerson of Brownstown, Indiana, was the Sixty-seventh's colonel and had by this time held that rank for all of nine days.

8. The "crackers" of Civil War soldiers were hardtack, an unleavened bread made of flour, water, and a bit of salt. Although many find its flavor not necessarily disagreeable, it is fairly bland and so hard that eating it requires either strong teeth or extreme ingenuity. Soldiers dunked it in their coffee, fried it in grease from their salt pork, or otherwise endeavored to enhance its palatability.

9. McDonough, *War in Kentucky*, 161–65.

10. McDonough, *War in Kentucky*, 165; Scott, *History of the 67th*, 7–8.

11. Scott, *History of the 67th*, 9.

12. McDonough, *War in Kentucky*, 172–83; *The War of the Rebellion: A Compilation of the Official Records of the Union and Confederate Armies* (Washington DC: GPO, 1880–1901), 16, pt. 1, 962 (hereafter OR).

13. Scott, *History of the 67th*, 9–10.

## 2. "The Grand Panorama before Me"

1. Scott, *History of the 67th*, 11–12.

2. See Mark Grimsley, *The Hard Hand of War: Union Military Policy toward Southern Civilians, 1861–1865* (New York: Cambridge University Press, 1995), 67–141.

3. The "Wes" to whom Winters frequently refers was his brother-in-law, Wesley Smith. He does not appear on the rolls of the Sixty-seventh Indiana and may have accompanied the regiment in some sort of unofficial capacity. *Report of the Adjutant General of the State of Indiana*, 8 vols. (Indianapolis: W. R. Holloway, 1865), 6:82–84.

4. By this time, the Sixty-seventh Indiana, along with the Sixteenth and Sixtieth Indiana, the Eighty-third and Ninety-sixth Ohio, and the Twenty-third Wisconsin, belonged to the brigade of Brig. Gen. S. G. Burbridge. Its division

*Notes to Pages*
*3–12*
{132}

would soon be incorporated into the Army of the Tennessee's Thirteenth Army Corps (Maj. Gen. John A. McClernand), when that organization was formed that winter. OR 24, pt. 1, 138.

5. Apparently the members of Winters's informal mess were paying him to do the cooking for the group. This was an ad hoc arrangement, worked out and financed by the soldiers themselves. The army had no regularly assigned cooks.

6. Pvt. William C. Everet, Company I, Sixty-seventh Indiana. The regimental records list Private Everet as "unaccounted for." *Report of the Adjutant General*, 8:270.

7. Hartsville, Indiana, is a small town in Bartholomew County, about forty miles southeast of Indianapolis.

8. Possibly Cpl. Reuben A. Blankenbeker, Company I, Sixty-seventh Indiana. He survived the war. *Report of the Adjutant General*, 6:82.

9. Pvt. Henry Case, Company I, Sixty-seventh Indiana, nevertheless survived the war. *Report of the Adjutant General*, 6:83.

10. Cpl. James Israel, Company I, Sixty-seventh Indiana. *Report of the Adjutant General*, 6:82.

11. On the subject of a good death and the importance of final messages from the departing, see Gerald F. Linderman, *Embattled Courage: The Experience of Combat in the American Civil War* (New York: Free Press, 1987), 29–31, 101, 109, 159, 248–49, and Reid Mitchell, *The Vacant Chair: The Northern Soldier Leaves Home* (New York: Oxford University Press, 1993), 139–44.

12. The steamboat *J. S. Pringle*, carrying the Sixty-seventh Indiana, was one of sixty transports used to carry Sherman's force down the river to Vicksburg. Charles Dana Gibson and E. Kay Gibson, *Assault and Logistics: Union Army Coastal and River Operations, 1861–1866*, The Army's Navy Series, volume 2 (Camden ME: Ensign Press, 1995), 152.

13. In the battle of Fredericksburg (Virginia), fought December 13, 1862, the Union Army of the Potomac under Ambrose Burnside suffered a lopsided defeat at the hands of Robert E. Lee's Army of Northern Virginia.

14. Pvt. John Gambold, Company I, Sixty-seventh Indiana. *Report of the Adjutant General*, 6:83.

15. Sgt. Fieldon McCalip, Company I, Sixty-seventh Indiana. *Report of the Adjutant General*, 6:82.

16. Friar's Point, Mississippi, was one of the many peninsulas formed by the various bends of the river. This one was on the east bank, between the west-bank towns of Helena and Napoleon, Arkansas.

17. The town of Napoleon, Arkansas, is located on the Mississippi River at the mouth of the Arkansas River.

18. "Seeing the elephant" was Civil War era slang for seeing or experiencing whatever great thing there was to be seen or experienced. It was usually used for

something more important than going ashore and looking around. In fact, it often referred to having the experience of combat, though that is obviously not what Winters means here.

19. Confederate cavalry leader Brig. Gen. Nathan Bedford Forrest. Winters was correct about Forrest not being in Memphis, but the wily Rebel had indeed been raiding, tearing up railroads and otherwise causing havoc, farther north in West Tennessee.

20. I.e., the colonel, still holding to the by this time outmoded approach to the war that forbade soldiers to forage off the civilian population, severely reprimanded and may have punished them.

21. Milliken's Bend was primarily the land on the Louisiana side within the broad loop of the Mississippi River that also bore that name, a few miles north of Vicksburg.

22. This was probably Pvt. Rosington Elms, Company C, Sixty-seventh Indiana. *Report of the Adjutant General*, 8:270.

23. Brig. Gen. Morgan Lewis Smith, who commanded the Second Division of the Fifteenth Corps, was seriously wounded at the battle of Chickasaw Bayou, December 28, 1862. Ezra J. Warner, *Generals in Blue: Lives of the Union Commanders* (Baton Rouge: Louisiana State University Press, 1964), 460.

24. Pvt. Charles McCombs, Company D, Sixty-seventh Indiana, is listed as having drowned in the Mississippi River, though the records give no date. He is probably the man to whom Winters refers here. *Report of the Adjutant General*, 8:273.

25. I.e., taking on wood as fuel for the steamboat.

26. In fact it was the Arkansas River and not the White.

27. That is, he listened to someone reading a newspaper. Civil War soldiers eagerly desired newspapers, and when one arrived in camp it was avidly read and shared with comrades, in this case even by reading aloud.

28. Whatever happened to Pvt. Richard Houser, Company C, Sixty-seventh Indiana, on this day to prompt Winters to mention his loss, he nevertheless remained with the regiment until its mustering out after the war. *Report of the Adjutant General*, 6:83.

### 3. "The Mournfull Call of the Sick"

1. Mitchell, *The Vacant Chair*, 75–87.

2. John William De Forest, *A Volunteer's Adventures: A Union Captain's Record of the Civil War*, ed. James H. Croushore (New Haven CT: Yale University Press, 1946), 151.

3. 1st Sgt. Joseph F. Carmichael, Company I, Sixty-seventh Indiana, was discharged April 10, 1863, because of disability caused by a wound. *Report of the Adjutant General*, 6:82.

4. The steamboat *Fanny Bullitt* had been chartered by the U.S. Army's quartermaster department as a transport late in 1861 or early in 1862. It had participated in Union operations on the Tennessee River, including the Fort Donelson and Shiloh campaigns, and most recently had brought the Sixteenth Ohio down the Mississippi as part of Sherman's late-1862 movement against Vicksburg and Arkansas Post. Gibson and Gibson, *Assault and Logistics*, 67, 79, 153.

5. Capt. Shepherd F. Eaton and 2d Lt. William H. Aikin were both from Hope, Indiana. Eaton resigned March 20, 1863. *Report of the Adjutant General*, 2:618.

6. The steamboat *J. J. Swan*, which was also sometimes called the *J. C. Swan*. Gibson and Gibson, *Assault and Logistics*, 79.

7. Pvt. Eli Zigler, Company I, Sixty-seventh Indiana. *Report of the Adjutant General*, 6:83.

8. Winters made a slight mistake in the direction of the sound, an understandable error from that distance. The action was in fact not on the Yazoo but on the Mississippi, where the Union ram *Queen of the West* made a daring daylight dash past the Confederate batteries at Vicksburg. It was on a mission to disrupt Southern use of the river between Vicksburg and Port Hudson, Louisiana, where another Confederate bastion held back Federal forces attempting to advance up the river from occupied New Orleans. OR 24, pt. 1, 336–39.

9. Of course this refers to the *Queen of the West*, mentioned in note 8, which ran the batteries alone.

10. I.e., ran down the Mississippi, past the Vicksburg batteries, into the crucial stretch of theoretically Confederate-controlled river south of Vicksburg and north of Port Hudson, Louisiana. In fact, after dark on the evening of February 13, a single ironclad gunboat, the U.S.S. *Indianola*, ran past the batteries, joining the unarmored ram U.S.S. *Queen of the West*, which had run the batteries on February 2. OR 24, pt. 1, 2.

11. Pvt. James Mobley, Company I, Sixty-seventh Indiana, is listed in the regiment's records as "unaccounted for." *Report of the Adjutant General*, 6:83, 8:273. Winters here supplies the information that Indiana's Adjutant General's Office lacked.

12. It probably meant nothing, being some incidental firing between batteries. The following day a skirmish occurred at Cypress Bend, Arkansas, when a reconnaissance expedition (including the Sixty-seventh Indiana) from Grant's army encountered Confederates, but this action involved little artillery and probably went unheard by Winters. OR 24, pt. 1, 349–52.

13. Winters was right to discount the rumor of his brigade's capture. It is probably a distorted account of the successful skirmish at Cypress Bend, Arkansas, mentioned in note 12.

14. Winters had his battles confused. The celebrated Mexican War victory he

names here, Monterey, was in fact fought September 20–24, 1846. An even more celebrated American victory, and the one Winters was thinking of, was the battle of Buena Vista, February 22, 1847.

15. Since the U.S. ram *Queen of the West* had run the Vicksburg batteries on February 2, it had been operating against Confederate shipping on the Mississippi and Red Rivers. On February 14, while engaging Confederate shore batteries in the Red River, the *Queen* ran aground (her commander said the fault lay with a disloyal pilot), had her steampipe severed by a Rebel shot, and was abandoned. She was subsequently repaired and taken into Confederate service. Winters was correct in assuming that the firing he had heard the night of the twentieth (the "night before last") was not related to the *Queen*. It was simply another exchange in the long semi-siege of Vicksburg, as Grant continued to look for a way to get his army behind Vicksburg and make the siege real.

16. Pvt. Parmenias H. Lick, Company I, Sixty-seventh Indiana. Curiously, the Indiana Adjutant General's records indicate that Lick died May 28, 1863, but Winters's account is more likely the accurate one in this case. *Report of the Adjutant General*, 6:83, 8:272. Regarding the manner of Lick's death, recent scholars of Civil War soldiering point out that such a passing, in which the sufferer did not know he was dying, was considered a very undesirable sort of death, in marked contrast to what people of the twentieth century might think. In the nineteenth century it was important that dying people knew they were dying and preferably were surrounded by family during the process, so that they might make some final statement to their loved ones and, most important, might prepare themselves, and give testimony of being prepared, for their impending meeting with God. See Reid Mitchell, *Civil War Soldiers* (New York: Viking, 1988), 60–64, and *The Vacant Chair*, 139–44, as well as Linderman, *Embattled Courage*, 29–31, 101, 109, 159, 248–49.

17. This is an attempt by Winters in some measure to compensate the family of young Lick for the extra pain in their bereavement caused by their absence from his dying bedside and the absence of any final statement from the deceased.

18. I.e., since Winters returned to the hospital February 13, after his brief stay with the regiment.

19. In fact, Winters was much deceived about the meanings of these night sounds. Below Vicksburg that night, four Confederate vessels attacked the *Indianola*. Among the attackers was the *Queen of the West*, captured after running aground on February 14. After a furious fight at close range, the commander of the *Indianola* surrendered his "partially sunken vessel." It was a major setback for the U.S. Navy in the war on the Mississippi River. Long and Long, *The Civil War Day By Day*, 322–23.

20. This was the expedition to Greenville, Mississippi, that had occasioned the skirmish at Cypress Bend, Arkansas, mentioned in note 12.

21. This is probably the Company I private listed in the regiment's records as Guane Gerret S. Dee (*Report of the Adjutant General*, 8:270) or Gerret S. Dee Gauno (6:83).

22. Pvt. William H. Burchfield (or Birchfield), Company I, Sixty-seventh Indiana, died in Memphis, date unknown. *Report of the Adjutant General*, 6:83, 8:269.

23. Pvt. Clinton Nelegh, Company I, Sixty-seventh Indiana. *Report of the Adjutant General*, 6:83, 8:273.

24. Brig. Gen. Stephen Gano Burbridge, Winters's brigade commander from his return to duty in late 1862 until early 1864. Warner, *Generals in Blue*, 54–55.

25. Thirteen dollars per month was the regular pay of Union army privates.

26. The "cut off" was an attempted canal across the base of De Soto Point, a peninsula on the Louisiana side of the Mississippi formed by a bend in the river immediately opposite Vicksburg. The idea was to divert the course of the Mississippi away from Vicksburg, thus canceling its strategic importance. Some of Grant's troops worked on the project throughout the winter, and Lincoln showed great interest in it. In the end, however, it came to nothing.

27. Dr. Charles S. Boynton of Hope, Indiana.

28. The steamboat *City of Memphis* had a Civil War career similar to that of the *Fanny Bullitt* (see note 4). It had been in charter to the army since at least November 1861, when it had carried troops in Grant's movement against Belmont. In the late-1862 movement down the Mississippi, it had carried a couple of batteries of artillery and a regiment of infantry. Gibson and Gibson, *Assault and Logistics*, 65, 67, 79, 153.

29. Indeed, Grant was beginning to make preparations for his bold spring campaign against the fortress town.

30. Grant had enjoyed no such success that day, but something far more colorful had occurred. For the second time in a matter of days, the Federals had sent floating down past Vicksburg an unmanned fake gunboat, that is, a raft cobbled up to look like one of the navy's western river gunboats. The Confederates were entirely taken in and shelled the bogus warship intensely.

31. The steamboat *Maria Denning*. Gibson and Gibson, *Assault and Logistics*, 560.

32. Apparently routine firing.

33. Though Grant was currently experimenting with an expedition through the waterway known as Yazoo Pass, this report of a great victory was, as Winters suspected, too good to be true. Nothing of the sort ever resulted from the Yazoo Pass expedition.

34. Varioloid was a mild form of small pox.

35. The previous night's firing had been occasioned when U.S. rear admiral David G. Farragut had run past the Confederate batteries at Grand Gulf, just below Vicksburg, with a small seagoing flotilla that had come all the way up the

Mississippi from the Gulf of Mexico. Long and Long, *The Civil War Day by Day*, 330.

36. This time Winters was mistaken. Brig. Gen. Willis A. Gorman, commanding the Union post at Helena, Arkansas, had not taken the key terrain at Haynes' Bluff, nor even tried for that matter. The firing Winters heard was simply more routine artillery sparring. OR 24, pt. 1, 67; Long and Long, *The Civil War Day by Day*, 330–31; Warner, *Generals in Blue*, 178–79; Stewart Sifakis, *Who Was Who in the Civil War* (New York: Facts on File, 1988).

37. A small settlement, no longer extant, near Milliken's Bend, on the Louisiana shore opposite Vicksburg.

38. Winters's division commander throughout the operations on the Mississippi was Brig. Gen. Andrew Jackson Smith.

39. The Western Sanitary Commission, midwestern counterpart to the eastern U.S. Sanitary Commission, was a relief organization dedicated to supplying what it could for the physical comfort of the soldiers, particularly the sick and wounded.

40. Probably Pvt. William C. Everet, Company I, Sixty-seventh Indiana. *Report of the Adjutant General*, 6:83, 8:270.

41. Columbus, Indiana, located on the Driftwood River, is the seat of Bartholomew County and lies about thirty-five miles south-southeast of Indianapolis.

42. Probably Pvt. William F. Maddex, Company I, Sixty-seventh Indiana. *Report of the Adjutant General*, 6:83, 8:272.

43. Sometime during the war, Pvt. Elijah Dudley, Company I, Sixty-seventh Indiana, died of disease. *Report of the Adjutant General*, 6:83, 8:270. He apparently recovered from the illness Winters mentions here, however, as he is mentioned in Winters's letter of April 14, 1863. See chapter 4.

44. Cpl. James Israel and Pvts. Charles S. Cook and Lewis Hedgecock, all of Company I, Sixty-seventh Indiana. No record exists of their mustering out or, for that matter, of anything else that may have happened to them after enlisting. *Report of the Adjutant General*, 6:82–83, 8:270, 272.

45. This is once again the Pvt. Gerret S. "Dee Gauno" of the Adjutant General's records (6:83; see also note 21 above).

46. Rear Adm. David D. Farragut was indeed anchored just below Vicksburg with two vessels of his seagoing naval squadron. On March 14, these two vessels, the *Albatross* and Farragut's flagship, the *Hartford*, had successfully run the Confederate batteries at Port Hudson, while the cannonade forced two other vessels back and destroyed another Federal warship. On March 18, Farragut took his small flotilla past the batteries at Grand Gulf and anchored below Vicksburg. Long and Long, *The Civil War Day by Day*, 328, 330.

47. Pvt. Clinton Nelegh, Company I, Sixty-seventh Indiana. *Report of the Adjutant General*, 6:83.

48. Pvt. George R. Oldam, Company H, and possibly Pvt. George W. Doan, Company G, Sixty-seventh Indiana. *Report of the Adjutant General*, 6:80, 82.

49. These five boats were the first of the specially altered armed transports of the Mississippi Marine Brigade, a special unit consisting of infantry, cavalry, and artillery intended to combat guerrillas along the river and keep it open and safe for Union shipping. See Gibson and Gibson, *Assault and Logistics*, 239–40.

50. Farragut's two vessels attacked the Confederate shore batteries at Warrenton, Mississippi, below Vicksburg, without decisive results. Long and Long, *The Civil War Day by Day*, 331.

51. Pvt. Frederick E. Bannus, Company I, Sixty-seventh Indiana. *Report of the Adjutant General*, 6:83.

52. Pvt. John Gambold, Company I, Sixty-seventh Indiana, died of disease in St. Louis, Missouri, March 17, 1863. *Report of the Adjutant General*, 8:271.

53. Pvt. John Burcham, Company I, Sixty-seventh Indiana. *Report of the Adjutant General*, 6:83, 8:269.

54. Capt. Shepherd F. Eaton, Company I, Sixty-seventh Indiana, resigned, March 20, 1863. *Report of the Adjutant General*, 2:618.

55. The subject of Winters's unflattering remarks, Pvt. Lewis Hedgecock, Company I, Sixty-seventh Indiana, may have been merely on leave, or he may have been discharged and then later reenlisted. In any case, according to the Indiana adjutant general's records, he was not mustered out of service until the end of the war (6:83). It is also entirely possible that the records are in error.

56. The reference here is to either John A. or Charles A. Reed, both privates in Company I. *Report of the Adjutant General*, 6:83.

57. Maj. Gen. Samuel Ryan Curtis commanded Union forces in Missouri and Arkansas.

58. The division was there all right, but it was a part of the Sixteenth Corps in Grant's army, not Curtis's trans-Mississippi forces, and its former commander, Maj. Gen. Charles Smith Hamilton, had in fact just submitted his resignation. Winters had apparently heard some incorrect army rumors. Warner, *Generals in Blue*, 199.

59. Probably Pvt. Benjamin F. Davenport, Company F, Sixty-seventh Indiana. *Report of the Adjutant General*, 6:78.

60. The "freak" to which Winters refers may have been the Democratic victory in the 1862 Congressional elections.

61. Sending the sick up the river to clear the hospitals was part of Grant's preparation for his major campaign of maneuver against Vicksburg.

62. This was, in fact, exactly what Grant planned and was even then in the process of undertaking. Elements of Winters's own Thirteenth Corps were at that moment marching toward New Carthage, Louisiana, on the Mississippi River below Vicksburg, where Grant envisioned crossing them to the Mis-

sissippi side for his campaign to take the fortress city. The Union commander would no doubt have been dismayed to have learned that his plans were being spelled out in such detail in the letter of a private soldier, hand-carried by a regimental sutler (i.e., a traveling civilian merchant attached to the military). Yet such shocking (by modern standards) breaches of security were the rule rather than the exception in the Civil War, and Winters broke no regulation and risked no punishment in sending such.

63. The town of Richmond, in Madison Parish, Louisiana, was seized by Union troops March 31, 1863, and lay along the route Grant's forces took in April of that year when they marched down the west side of the river to cross below Vicksburg.

## 4. "We Whiped the Rebels Badly"

1. Pvt. Michael Lewis, Company I, Sixty-seventh Indiana. *Report of the Adjutant General*, 6:83, 8:272.

2. Doctors James Dodd of Harrodsburg, Indiana, and George W. Bryan of Bloomington were the two assistant surgeons then serving with the Sixty-seventh Indiana. *Report of the Adjutant General*, 2:615.

3. This is the letter of March 21, 1863, printed in chapter 3.

4. Assistant Surgeon James Dodd resigned his commission effective April 11, 1863. *Report of the Adjutant General*, 2:615.

5. Hinds County, Mississippi, includes the state capital of Jackson and the country just to the west of it, roughly between the Big Black River, on the west, and the Pearl River, on the east.

6. At the battle of Port Gibson, Mississippi, May 1, 1863, the Sixty-seventh was heavily engaged, and Winters's own Company I was in the thick of the fighting as skirmishers for the regiment. OR 24, pt. 1, 593–94.

7. The battle of Raymond, Mississippi, May 12, 1863.

8. Dr. Charles S. Boynton of Hope, Indiana, later became the chief surgeon of the Sixty-seventh Indiana, serving from April 1864 until the end of the war. *Report of the Adjutant General*, 2:614.

9. Winters's reference to a night march preceding the battle, with the Sixty-seventh arriving on the field early in the morning, describes the regiment's approach to the battlefield of Port Gibson, eleven days earlier. Winters must have gotten separated from his regiment somewhat, for their involvement in the battle of Port Gibson was not that of a reserve regiment. Also, two members of Company B were wounded at the outset of the battle. OR 24, pt. 1, 593–94.

10. Pvt. Eli Zigler, Company I, Sixty-seventh Indiana, *Report of the Adjutant General*, 6:83, 270.

11. Pvt. Elijah Dudley, Company I, Sixty-seventh Indiana, *Report of the Adjutant General*, 6:83, 270.

12. This, of course, is once again Winters's close friend Pvt. Charles L. Bannus of Company I, Sixty-seventh Indiana. Bannus survived the war. *Report of the Adjutant General*, 6:83.

13. Private Henry Bruner, Company I, Sixty-seventh Indiana. The Indiana adjutant general's records state that Bruner was killed at Vicksburg in May 1863 (6:83, 8:269).

14. Cpl. Charles Riley, Company I, Sixty-seventh Indiana. Riley survived the war and was mustered out as a sergeant in July 1865. *Report of the Adjutant General*, 6:82.

15. Pvt. John A. Crisler, Company I, Sixty-seventh Indiana. Like Riley, Crisler finished the war as a sergeant. *Report of the Adjutant General*, 6:83.

16. Pvt. William Blair, Company I, Sixty-seventh Indiana, served out the remainder of the war. *Report of the Adjutant General*, 6:83.

17. Besides Winters's friend Bannus, these are Sgt. Fieldon McCalip and Pvt. Thomas V. Eaton, Company C, Sixty-seventh Indiana. *Report of the Adjutant General*, 6:82–83.

18. Assistant Surgeons James Dodd and George W. Bryan resigned April 11 and May 27, respectively. Rather than return to the regiment after his furlough, Surgeon James W. F. Gerish resigned August 13. William A. Burton was commissioned as an assistant surgeon on May 29. Dean's name does not appear in the adjutant general's records at all. *Report of the Adjutant General*, 2:614–15.

19. The major assault on May 22, 1863.

20. Emanuel Sawers, Jacob F. Shutt, and Levi Snyder, all privates in Company I, Sixty-seventh Indiana. *Report of the Adjutant General*, 6:83.

21. This is a strange new concern for military secrecy, given Winters's previous explanation of Grant's campaign plan on the eve of its execution. Possibly an alert regimental officer decided it was time to monitor the flow of information or at least admonished the men to caution. In any case, Grant seems to have had no established policy of censoring soldiers' letters. In that era such a thing would have been well-nigh unthinkable politically.

22. George W. Friedly, of Hope, Indiana, was promoted to captain of Company I upon the resignation of Shepherd F. Eaton from the position, March 21, 1863. *Report of the Adjutant General*, 2:614.

23. William H. Aikin of Hope, Indiana, was promoted from second to first lieutenant, Company I, when First Lieutenant Friedly moved up to fill Eaton's place. *Report of the Adjutant General*, 2:614.

24. Pvt. Henry S. Shultz, Company I, Sixty-seventh Indiana. *Report of the Adjutant General*, 6:83.

25. Both that day, Wednesday, June 17, and the previous Sunday, June 14, were routine days during the Vicksburg siege. Long and Long, *The Civil War Day by Day*, 365–66, 368.

26. On this day Union army and navy guns did indeed launch an unusually heavy artillery bombardment, lasting six hours. Long and Long, *The Civil War Day by Day*, 369.

27. Maj. Gen. Joseph Hooker, commanding the Army of the Potomac, had made an attempt to take Richmond in May but had been defeated by Robert E. Lee at Chancellorsville.

28. Wilson was not an officer in the Sixty-seventh Indiana.

## 5. "*Vicksburgh Is Ours!*"

1. Winters may not have been aware of it, but scurvy is caused by dietary deficiency (lack of vitamin C). The Confederates, who had been on extremely short rations, including as Winters stated, mule meat, could have been expected to have had a great deal of scurvy.

2. Pvt. Joseph Gambold, Company I, Sixty-seventh Indiana, served through the duration of the war. *Report of the Adjutant General*, 6:84.

3. Confederate general Joseph E. Johnston, having failed in his assigned task of raising the siege of Vicksburg, fell back into the pine woods of east-central Mississippi.

4. In late June, Confederate cavalry leader Brig. Gen. John H. Morgan set out with two thousand men on a raid that took him northward from Middle Tennessee across Kentucky. On July 8, Morgan and his men crossed the Ohio River west of Louisville, to the consternation of citizens in the midwestern states. He passed about twenty miles to the south of Winters's home in Hope, Indiana, as he progressed northeastward, crossing the Ohio line at Harrison on July 13. During his course through Indiana, Morgan was seriously harassed, though not stopped, by a number of Indiana militia and home guard units.

5. This "Mr. Allen," or "Frank," is probably Musician Benjamin F. Allen, Company I, Sixty-seventh Indiana. *Report of the Adjutant General*, 6:83.

6. This may be a reference to the Winters's former residence in Cincinnati.

7. Pvt. Mason Lawless, Company I, Sixty-seventh Indiana, later died in Memphis. *Report of the Adjutant General*, 6:272.

8. Pvt. William F. Maddex, Company I, Sixty-seventh Indiana, *Report of the Adjutant General*, 6:83.

9. Pvt. Emanuel Sawers, Company I, Sixty-seventh Indiana, nevertheless managed to serve out the duration of the war. *Report of the Adjutant General*, 6:83.

10. In fact, although Morgan was defeated in a skirmish at Buffinton's Island on July 18 and seven hundred of his men were captured, the wily raider himself fled northeastward and was not finally captured until July 26, the very day Winters wrote this letter.

11. Sgt. Fieldon McCalip, Company I, Sixty-seventh Indiana, *Report of the Adjutant General*, 6:82.

12. Port Hudson, Louisiana, was, like Vicksburg, an important Confederate bastion on the Mississippi River. It surrendered on July 8, 1863.

13. The steamboat *City of Madison* was among at least ten vessels known to have been destroyed by a group of Confederate civilian arsonists operating under the auspices of the Confederate War Department. Gibson and Gibson, *Assault and Logistics*, 244–45.

## 6. "Down the River"

1. Pvt. Henry S. Shultz or Henry S. Shutz, Company I, Sixty-seventh Indiana. *Report of the Adjutant General*, 6:82, 86.

2. On September 8 Union naval and land forces, under the overall direction of Banks and the immediate command of Maj. Gen. William B. Franklin, failed in an effort to take Sabine Pass, on the gulf coast at the mouth of the Sabine River, between Texas and Louisiana.

3. The provost marshall's—that is, the officer in charge of maintaining order and discipline within a rear area. This department was similar to the modern military police.

4. Pvt. Jacob F. Shutt, Company I, Sixty-seventh Indiana. *Report of the Adjutant General*, 6:83.

5. The regiment had marched westward through Louisiana with Maj. Gen. William B. Franklin's ill-fated Bayou Teche expedition. For more information on the expedition, see Richard Lowe's *The Texas Overland Expedition of 1863* (Fort Worth TX: Ryan Place, 1996).

6. On November 3, 1863, the Sixty-seventh Indiana formed part of the rear guard of Franklin's failed Bayou Teche expedition as it withdrew toward New Orleans. Confederate forces who had harassed the rear guard for several days struck suddenly and caught the Federals by surprise at Bayou Bourbeau. The fighting was intense and became hand-to-hand at times. The Confederates lost 125 men killed and wounded to 154 such for the Federals. However, 562 additional Union soldiers (including about 200 of approximately 300 members present of the Sixty-seventh) were taken prisoner. One member of the Sixty-seventh estimated that only about 70 men of the regiment escaped. Scott, *History of the 67th*, 51–52; Lowe, *The Texas Overland Expedition*, 63–104.

7. Probably Pvt. Christopher Hiniger, Company I, Sixty-seventh Indiana. All the regimental rolls were, of course, written out by hand, sometimes by indifferent penmen, often under circumstances disadvantageous for writing. As a result, mistranscriptions and garbled names are not unusual. *Report of the Adjutant General*, 6:83.

8. Pvt. Owen Billard, Company I, Sixty-seventh Indiana. *Report of the Adjutant General*, 6:83.

9. Capt. George R. Sims of Columbus, Indiana. *Report of the Adjutant General*, 2:616.

10. As Winters feared, his captured comrades did have to face hard forced marches, rough treatment, and scant fare until they were paroled December 31, 1863. Some did not survive. Contrary to Winters's expectation, however, Lieutenant Aikins did survive and went on to become captain of Company I of the Twenty-fourth Indiana when it and the Sixty-seventh were consolidated near the end of the war. The members of the Sixty-seventh who were paroled in December were not exchanged until the following June and therefore did not take part in the spring 1864 Red River Campaign. Scott, *History of the 67th*, 62–64; *Report of the Adjutant General*, 2:618.

11. The town of Brashear City, now Morgan City, lay in St. Mary's Parish in extreme southern Louisiana, just southeast of Berwick, on the west bank of the Atchafalaya River.

12. New Iberia is a town in Iberia Parish in south-central Louisiana, about fifteen miles from the sea.

13. Aside from Captain Friedly, the soldiers mentioned here are Pvts. Lewis Hine, John Hedgecock, Ezra Reed, Emanuel Sawers, William A. Covert, John Clark, and Henry S. Shultz or Shutz, all of Company I. Isaac Stuckey does not appear in any of the records of the Sixty-seventh Indiana. *Report of the Adjutant General*, 6:83, 86.

14. Col. Frank Emerson of Brownstown, Indiana, was the Sixty-seventh's first and only full colonel. He was just returning to the regiment at this time after recuperating from a wound sustained at Arkansas Post in January 1863. *Report of the Adjutant General*, 2:614; Scott, *History of the 67th*, 66.

15. Maj. Gen. Nathaniel P. Banks was commander of the Department of the Gulf.

16. In the battle of Chattanooga, November 23–25, 1863, the Union forces of Ulysses S. Grant had indeed decisively defeated the Confederate Army of Tennessee under Braxton Bragg, but it would be another nine months before Atlanta fell.

17. A "shebang" (or "chebang" as Winters spells it here) was what the Civil War soldier called a hut he or his fellow soldiers built, usually as their winter quarters.

18. Algiers, Louisiana, was located on the west bank of the Mississippi opposite New Orleans.

### 7. "This Delectable Point of Sand"

1. Winters was once again the victim of exaggerated camp rumors, for no significant action had taken place at Indianola that day or for some time before.

The firing he heard represented incidental skirmishing that never made it into the official reports.

2. Brig. Gen. Thomas Edward Greenfield Ransom.

3. That is, Carion Crow Bayou, by which Winters refers to the battle of Bayou Bourbeau, where much of his regiment was captured.

4. Union draft law provided that conscription would go into effect in a given district if that area failed to meet a specified quota of volunteer recruiting.

5. Pvt. Henry S. Shultz, Company I, Sixty-seventh Indiana. *Report of the Adjutant General*, 6:83.

6. As the crow flies, it is just under one thousand miles from Point Cavallo, Texas, to Hope, Indiana. Winters apparently was not well acquainted with any crows and had gotten some figures for the roundabout route by ship through the Gulf of Mexico, then up the Mississippi by steamboat to Cairo, and thence by railroad to Indianapolis and overland down to Hope.

7. Galveston, Texas, had changed hands several times during the war but had been held by the Confederates since January 1, 1863, and continued in their hands until the end of the war.

8. From January 21 to 25, 1864, General Ransom took the First Brigade, Fourth Division, Thirteenth Corps, commanded by Col. W. J. Landram (including Winters and the Sixty-seventh Indiana), along with two batteries of artillery, on a reconnaissance expedition up the Matagorda Peninsula. The first day they marched 14 miles, the next 22. The third day they marched another 17 miles and skirmished with Confederate troops, who threatened to meet them in force. Having gained much valuable information, they marched back on January 24 and 25, covering 106 miles round trip. OR 34, pt. 1, 99–100.

9. In fact, the opposite shore was a good deal closer than that. A march of fifty-two miles from Point Cavallo would have taken the brigade nearly to where the Matagorda Peninsula joins the mainland. For most of the hike (after the first ten or fifteen miles), the troops would have been within about five miles of the mainland.

10. Either this date or the date on the previous letter is incorrect. The contents indicate that the two letters were written on different days, probably two or three days apart.

11. Pvt. Lewis Hine, Company I, Sixty-seventh Indiana. *Report of the Adjutant General*, 8:275.

12. Maj. Gen. Edward O. C. Ord had recently taken command of the Thirteenth Corps.

13. Maj. Gen. Napoleon Jackson Tecumseh Dana had commanded the Thirteenth Corps's Second Division for the last three months of 1863 and had acted as corps commander for two of those months. Early in January 1864 he had turned over corps command to Ord and also relinquished his division command. In March he was assigned to lead the corps's First Division.

1. The town of Berwick is located in St. Mary Parish in southern Louisiana, about fifteen miles from Atchafalaya Bay, a part of the Gulf of Mexico.

2. This sentence refers to Atchafalaya Bay, on the Gulf coast, whence the ships proceeded up the Atchafalaya River to Berwick Bay, a small, semi-landlocked body of water in the midst of the swamps of southern Louisiana.

3. Franklin, Louisiana, was actually only about twenty-five miles away. It lay on the banks of Bayou Teche, which would be the expedition's route during the first part of its journey.

4. Historian of the Red River Campaign Ludwell Johnson describes this stretch of Bayou Teche, "with its deep placid water and graceful curves, winding through level fields that before war came had been thick with sugar cane. Great live oaks and orange groves surrounded the mansions of planters who not too many months ago had been the lords of creation in their particular corner of the world." Ludwell H. Johnson, *Red River Campaign: Politics and Cotton in the Civil War* (Baltimore: Johns Hopkins University Press, 1958), 98–100, quote on p. 99.

5. This is a reference to the large reenlistment bounties then being offered to entice the continued service of soldiers whose regiments, unlike the Sixty-seventh Indiana, had formed in 1861 and thus were nearing the end of their three-year term of enlistment.

6. 2d Lt. William M. Friedly, of Hope, Indiana, and Company I, Sixty-seventh Indiana, resigned February 17, 1864. *Report of the Adjutant General*, 2:619.

7. Maj. Gen. Andrew Jackson Smith was attached to Banks's Red River Expedition with a detachment from the Army of the Tennessee, two divisions of the Sixteenth Corps and one of the Seventeenth Corps.

8. Pvt. Clinton Nelegh (or Neligh) was mustered into Company I when the regiment was organized in August 1862, but his brother, Solon, was mustered in as a recruit January 27, 1864. Clinton had obviously been absent from the regiment for some time prior to this. He had probably been discharged and then reenlisted, since his name appears on the rolls both as an original member of the company and as a recruit mustered in on the same day as his brother. *Report of the Adjutant General*, 6:83–84.

9. George Hansen does not appear on the rolls of the Sixty-seventh Indiana. *Report of the Adjutant General*, 6:71–84.

10. Johnson, *Red River Campaign*, 124–26; OR 34, pt. 1, 220–29; Scott, *The History of the 67th*, 70.

11. OR 34, pt. 1, 296, 298; *Report of the Adjutant General*, 2:614; Scott, *History of the 67th*, 70.

12. OR 34, pt. 1, 290; Scott, *History of the 67th*, 70.

13. OR 34, pt. 1, 290–99; Scott, *History of the 67th*, 70–71; Johnson, *Red River Campaign*, 127–28.

14. OR 34, pt. 1, 264–66, 290–99; Scott, *History of the 67th*, 71; Johnson, *Red River Campaign*, 128.

15. OR 34, pt. 1, 264–68, 290–99, 462; Scott, *History of the 67th*, 71–72.

16. OR 34, pt. 1, 267, 292.

17. OR 34, pt. 1, 264–68, 296–97, 462; Scott, *History of the 67th*, 72.

18. Johnson, *Red River Campaign*, 131–287.

19. OR 34, pt. 1, 292.

20. Cpl. Bartimas Burk, Company I, Sixty-seventh Indiana, survived the war. *Report of the Adjutant General*, 6:83.

21. No soldier of this name appears on the official rolls of the Sixty-seventh Indiana. *Report of the Adjutant General*, 6:71–86.

22. Pvt. George Shuck had joined the regiment January 29, 1864. His fate is officially listed as "unaccounted for." *Report of the Adjutant General*, 6:86, 8:275.

23. Linderman, *Embattled Courage*, 248–49.

# INDEX